Reading Round Edinburgh

Reading Round Edinburgh

A Guide to Children's Books of the City

Edited by Lindsey Fraser and Kathryn Ross

Floris Books

Illustrations by Adrian B. McMurchie

First published in 2007 by Floris Books
© Lindsey Fraser and Kathryn Ross
Introduction © J.K. Rowling

The publisher acknowledges a grant from the
Scottish Arts Council towards this publication.

British Library CIP Data available

ISBN 978-086315-593-2

Produced by Polskabook, Poland

Contents

NEXT PAGE: Inside the Scott Monument

Introduction
by J.K. Rowling

All writers dread the question "where do you get your ideas from?" Agatha Christie wrote that she longed to snap back "at the Army and Navy Store." Once, in my annoying ex-teacher way, I turned the question back on a boy at a book reading. "Well, I get my ideas the same way that you get yours. Where do your ideas come from?" "I never have ideas," he said, apparently quite sincerely, to gales of laughter.

I cannot be sure whether I would have had different ideas for the Harry Potter books if I had written them in cafés all over Birmingham or Bristol, but I suspect that I would. If you spend a lot of time walking around a city while sorting through your ideas, the things that you see and experience as you go must permeate your thoughts. It is, however, the conscious memories of Edinburgh that leap out of the pages of Harry Potter for me: the places I wrote particular chapters and passages; where I despaired of ever having another idea; where I experienced all the delights and the frustrations of living in a fictional world. My love affair with writing in this city culminated in having the book launch of the sixth Harry Potter at Edinburgh Castle, easily my favourite launch so far.

The three years I spent living in Leith were difficult in many ways, and yet my heart lifts every time I drive down Leith Walk. I walked home along that street so many times, sometimes elated after a really good writing day, bolstered by my passionate belief in Harry Potter and refusing, unless at my lowest moments, to admit the possibility that nothing would ever come of it. It was in our flat at the bottom of Leith Walk that I found out that I was going to be published. I have only been back to see that flat once since I moved out, and I burst into tears at the sight of it and cried uncontrollably all the way back home. My husband, who was with me, was a little disconcerted; all I knew was that my life changed forever beyond those curtains. To this day I feel as though a bit of me is still living in South Lorne Place.

I remember sitting on the restaurant boat in Leith Docks with my old friend from university, Pauline, who was up for a visit. I was midway through my first ever week of serious press attention, and I carry an

indelible image of Pauline beaming at me, proud and excited on my behalf, while I felt uncomfortable and exposed, and assumed the fuss would be over in a couple of days.

I remember wandering around the National Gallery of Scotland in 1997 during my only serious (to date — must not get too complacent) bout of writer's block. This was a rather desperate and random measure inspired by the fact that I knew that Iris Murdoch and John Bailey had taken to wandering art galleries to shift a similar creative block. I don't think it worked for Iris and it definitely didn't work for me; I remember staring at Gainsborough's portrait of Mrs Graham, feeling utterly miserable and wishing I could change places with her.

But most of all, there are the cafés. I arrived in Edinburgh after a few years in Oporto, where the climate is ideally suited to a café culture. Now I was no longer writing on pavements in bright sunlight, but in warm, often smoky, rooms with rain beating at the windows.

My beloved Nicolsons, which used to be opposite the Festival Theatre, is no more. There was no better writing table in the world than the corner table at Nicolsons, with its wonderful view of people and traffic stretching away down Nicolson Street and the Bridges. That was where I wrote the single most effortless chapter of the whole Harry Potter series (chapter ten, *Philosopher's Stone*), almost in one go, while my daughter Jessica slept in her pushchair behind me. In my study at home, now, is the only surviving bunch of the papier-mâché flowers that used to decorate Nicolsons' walls, given to me by my brother-in-law, one of the co-owners, shortly after he told me they were selling. He was glad to be moving on, looking forward to the next venture, so I tried not to be too maudlin, but in fact I felt as though they were bulldozing my maternity hospital.

I used to love writing in the Elephant House, on George IV Bridge, but those days are long gone; they've put up a truly awful picture of me in the window, and not fancying being identified as the original, I stay away. But I still write in other Edinburgh cafés, where the staff know exactly what I'll order because I am such a creature of habit when it comes to writing. I sometimes see them smiling at me indulgently when I look up, searching for inspiration in the gleam of the espresso machine. Two weeks ago, while mentally groping for an appropriate Christian name for a character, a waitress bent over me with the perfect solution pinned to the front of her T-shirt. I must remember to drop in a complimentary copy once the book's finished.

Foreign journalists, particularly if wanting to film me, are usually thrilled by Edinburgh's cobbled streets, its winding alleys and looming, dramatic castle. The city offers many Potter-esque vistas, and I know I sometimes disappoint when I say that I cannot point to any building or streets that have a direct counterpart in my fictional world. However, I am not always believed when I say this. A man who worked at a certain public school in Edinburgh once wrote to invite me to look around, as I had "clearly" based Hogwarts upon his workplace. I wrote back politely to thank him for the invitation, but added truthfully that I had been writing about Hogwarts for four years before I ever set eyes on his school. I thought that would be the last I heard of him, but I was wrong; within days, he wrote back to tell me that I was mistaken, and that I had definitely based Hogwarts on his school. The correspondence ended at that point, so I don't know whether he is still telling people that he works at the "real" Hogwarts: I suspect he is.

© J.K. Rowling, 2007

1. Edinburgh

Like all cities, Edinburgh is the result of thousands of stories — some imagined, some remembered and retold, some long-forgotten.

Hills dominate the city and its horizons. There are the sweeping Pentlands to the south, sedate city hills at Blackford, Craiglockhart and Corstorphine, and Holyrood Park's dramatic Salisbury Crags, which together with Arthur's Seat provide a dramatic backdrop to the Palace of Holyrood at the foot of the Royal Mile. Looking out from Edinburgh Castle, which is perched on an extinct volcano, to the north, beyond the waters of the Firth of Forth, you can see the Lomonds in Fife, and on a good day, look for the Sidlaws in Perthshire. The Ochils sit behind Stirling, announcing the beginning of the Scottish Highlands, and on a spectacularly clear day, look north-west towards Ben Lomond, the Cobbler and Ben Ledi, east towards the Lammermuirs, and south again towards the Moorfoots leading towards the Borders.

But this book is about views within in the city: the passing of a maroon-coloured Edinburgh bus; a small

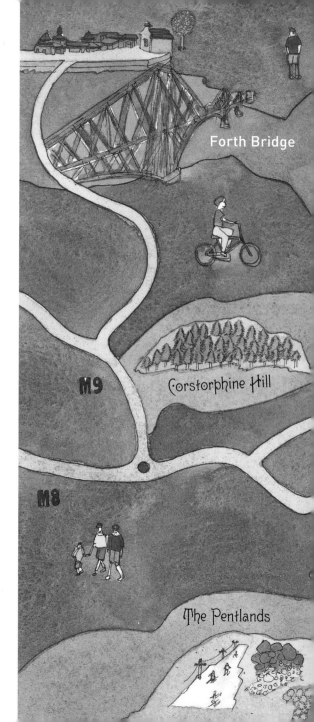

Forth Bridge

Corstorphine Hill

M9

M8

The Pentlands

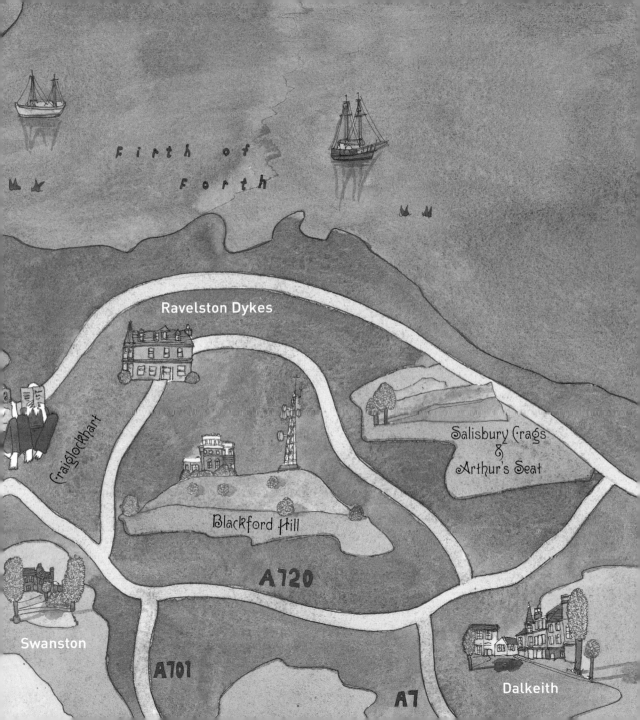

This is a true story by one of Edinburgh's resident writers, Janey Louise Jones, recalling her youngest son's imagination on a hot summer's day.

Dressed as a soldier in camouflage fatigues and helmet, seven year-old Louis asked to climb to the top of Arthur's Seat.

He was on a mission to conquer the enemy and reach the top of the world.

The brave commando set out fearlessly. He ran ahead in order to ambush me at intervals, gleeful in his childish sense of invincibility and supremacy.

But suddenly, the mood changed as we were both met by the alarming sight of flames raging across the blackened gorse.

Louis was afraid, suddenly a tiny child once more.

"Mummy, is the volcano erupting again?" he asked with terror in his voice.

statue of a dog; shops amongst narrow streets lined with tenements; tourists on a hot summer's evening. These small sights, and the sounds that accompany them, are the lifeblood of many of the Edinburgh writers you will encounter in this book.

While most of us make our way to the shops, school, cinema or local library without taking time to look around, writers watch and take note. And the stories we find in our bookshops and libraries are inevitably influenced by some of what they see.

2. From the Castle to the Tron

The writer and children's book consultant Valerie Bierman describes a walk she has taken many times with her children and now her grandchildren:

Turn your back on Edinburgh Castle with its thousand years of history. Walk down from the Esplanade — home of the famous Edinburgh Military Tattoo every August. At the top of the Royal Mile is the Lawnmarket, packed with history and incident, which inspired many of the scenes in Mollie Hunter's historical thrillers. The Lawnmarket was nothing to do with grass or gardens — it was originally a market where linen (or lawn) was sold.

To the left through Lady Stair's Close, named after a certain Lady Elizabeth Stair, who once lived in the close, is Lady Stair's House, now the Writers' Museum. Here, you'll find out about the lives of Robert Burns, Sir Walter Scott and Robert Louis Stevenson — writers who are still famous throughout the world.

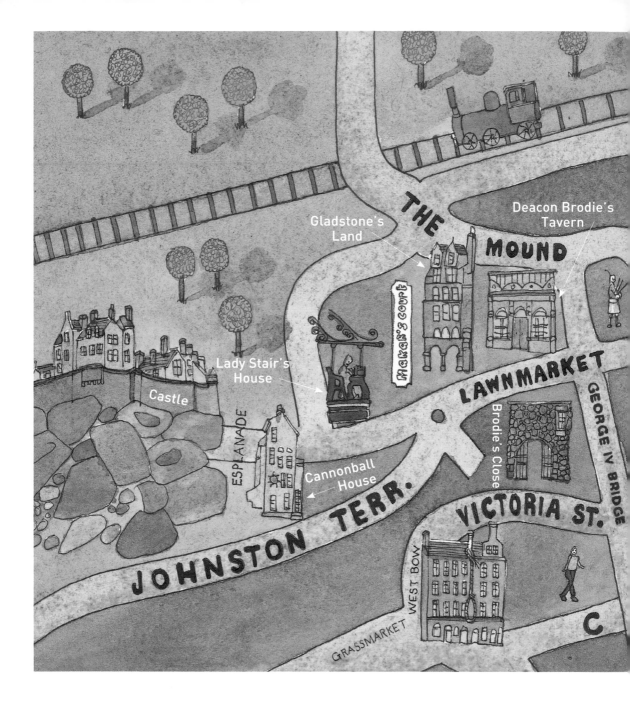

Gladstone's Land

Deacon Brodie's Tavern

THE MOUND

Lady Stair's House

Makar's Court

Castle

LAWNMARKET

Brodie's Close

ESPLANADE

GEORGE IV BRIDGE

Cannonball House

JOHNSTON TERR.

VICTORIA ST.

WEST BOW

GRASSMARKET

C

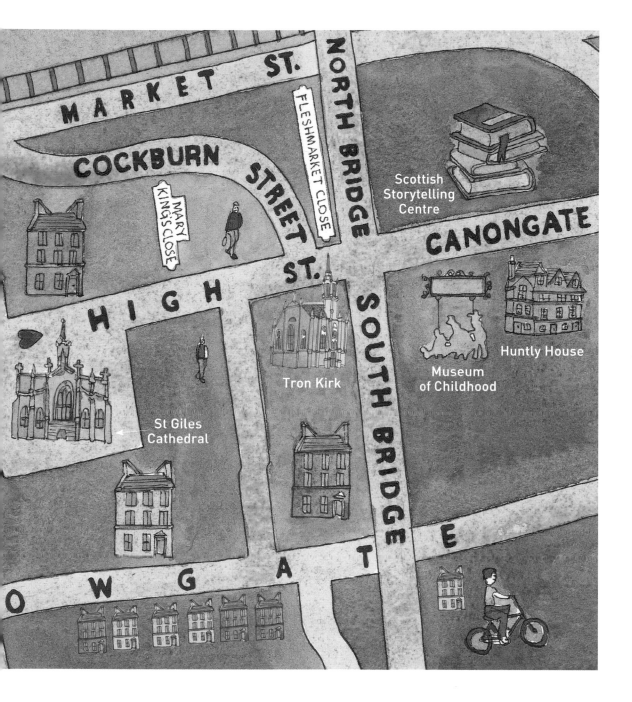

MARKET ST.

COCKBURN STREET ST.

NORTH BRIDGE

FLESHMARKET CLOSE

MARY KINGS CLOSE

Scottish
Storytelling
Centre

CANONGATE

HIGH

Huntly House

Museum
of Childhood

Tron Kirk

St Giles
Cathedral

SOUTH BRIDGE

E

O   W   G   A   T

You get a real feel for the way they lived. I've always been transfixed by Stevenson's boots — he must have had enormous feet!

Look for the quotations from all three in the courtyard outside — Makar's Court. "Makar" is the Scots word for a poet or bard.

I love historical novels. When I look around the narrow closes and up at the towering tenements, I am reminded of Iona McGregor's *An Edinburgh Reel* and Joan Lingard's *The Sign of the Black Dagger* — books in which old Edinburgh comes alive. Gladstone's Land, named after Thomas Gladstanes, a prosperous merchant who bought it in 1617, is a perfectly preserved seventeenth-century tenement. Land is the old name for an Edinburgh tenement — the grander you were, the higher up you lived to escape the stench from the street.

From *The Spanish Letters* by Mollie Hunter:

The Englishman craned upwards at the tall housefronts. "You build high in Edinburgh," he remarked.

"There is no room to build outwards and we are to keep safe within the city walls," Jamie told him seriously.

"Safe from whom?" The Englishman tossed the query out lightly, smiling again as he dismounted and handed the reins for Jamie to hold. For a second the boy hesitated in face of that friendly smile, but the habit of forthright speech was strong upon him.

"The English," he said bluntly.

Brodie's Close, on the right, and Deacon Brodie's Tavern on the corner of the High Street and the Mound, commemorate William Brodie, a skilled carpenter who invented a new type of scaffold — and was the first person to be hanged on it in 1788! Most people believe that Robert Louis Stevenson used Brodie as the inspiration for his book, *The Strange Case of Dr Jekyll and Mr Hyde*.

Keith Gray, a writer who revels in mysteries and intrigue, is fascinated by that particular book.

Keith Gray asks, What do the Incredible Hulk, Darth Vader and Dr Jekyll and Mr Hyde have in common? Edinburgh, obviously.

In the mid-eighteenth century, one of Edinburgh's most notorious figures was Deacon Brodie. He was a respectable cabinet-maker by day, but a villainous housebreaker by night. He used his day-job as cover for spying out the best houses to burgle. Afterwards, he would lavish his ill-gotten gains in the howffs of the Old Town — and so would no doubt be pleased that a pub on the Royal Mile now bears his name.

Stevenson knew the story of the two-faced Brodie from an early age because in his bedroom was a chest of drawers made by the man. And if Brodie inspired Jekyll and Hyde, then Stevenson's classic chiller has also inspired many films and books about characters torn between their good and evil natures — including angry, green superheroes and fallen Jedi Knights.

Look right towards the austere façade of the National Library of Scotland, a remarkable place storing thousands of books. Publishers are supposed to send one free copy of every book they publish there.

Nicola Morgan set her novel, *Fleshmarket,* in nineteenth-century Edinburgh, and visited the National Library during her research.

This was where I, a non-historian, first felt the power of history. In a special room, a man with white gloves carefully set a large folder on a soft cream pillow. Were my hands clean? I mustn't hold a pencil while I touched the yellowed pages. And so, hardly breathing, I began to read the newspapers from the trial of Burke and Hare, eye-witness accounts, real letters from real people — on paper they had touched. And suddenly, I was there, not reading a history book but touching history.

Just before you reach St Giles, you'll see a heart-shaped design in the cobbles. This marks the place where the Old Tolbooth, Edinburgh's notorious prison, stood until 1817. Nicknamed "The Heart of Midlothian" it was a grim place. There's an unsavoury tradition of spitting on the Heart for

Nicola Morgan

Mollie Hunter

good luck. One explanation is that criminals used to spit on the Tolbooth door as they passed. Of course these days, if you're a football fan, Heart of Midlothian means something entirely different.

The Tolbooth provides an important backdrop for Mollie Hunter's *The Lothian Run*.

It was on a September night in 1736 that the whole city of Edinburgh rose in riot — but not in the usual haphazard sort of way. In "The Porteous Riot," as this one came to be called, it seemed that someone had secretly organized the mob into a disciplined army that first of all took control of the city itself, so making sure that no outside force could be brought in to stop them storming the Tolbooth, which housed the town jail, and dragging out from there to his death a man called Porteous.

So who was that "someone?" Why would he have organized that attack on the jail? And what had that to do with a certain George Robertson who, besides being a mortal enemy of Porteous, was also a notorious smuggler on the run from the law?

To this day, you can walk the very streets where the violent action of that riot took place. In the one called West

From *The Lothian Run*
by Mollie Hunter:

"A monstrous-looking creation!" Gilmour's gaze shifted from the bustle in the Lawnmarket to the Tolbooth towering above it, and he slowed his pace the better to examine the structure of the jail.

As black and grim-looking as any building of its purpose could be, it stood right in the path of the High Street's traffic, which had to divide to flow through a narrow alley on one side of it and a rather broader one on the other. A row of ramshackle buildings several storeys high leaned crazily against its western wall, with shops of various kinds occupying their ground floors. Ribbons, gloves, and other trifles were the kind of goods on display there, and with amusement Gilmour noted the brisk trade being done by the vendors of the gew-gaws.

"A strange place to come for the purchase of folderols," he said, smiling.

Bow, you can even visit the shop where that "someone" bought the rope that would hang Porteous. Yet why did he reward the shopkeeper for that with a golden coin instead of the few pence it should have cost?

The mystery behind all this has never been solved — except perhaps in my book, *The Lothian Run*.

St Giles Cathedral stands on a spot that has been used for religious gatherings for over one thousand years. Giles, a seventh-century hermit, was said to have been wounded accidentally by a huntsman and, if you look above the main west door, you will see him shielding a deer.

The Cathedral is full of stories; the best known is about John Knox whose sermon, in 1560, led to the Reformation, dramatically changing religion in Scotland. In the years that followed you might have found a fire station, school, shops and even a prison there. In the eighteenth century, St Giles was surrounded by "luckenbooths" — small stalls nestling close to the walls selling gold, books

and fine fabrics. Sometimes stalls are still set up at weekends, but with less exotic items for sale! Mollie Hunter recalls how the bells of St Giles were used to raise the alarm in the seventeenth century.

From *The Thirteenth Member* by Mollie Hunter:

"You — rouse the Lord Provost, and give my warrant to raise the hue and cry. You — rouse the Dean of Guild and charge him bring out the craftsmen flying their banner of the Blue Blanket, every man armed with the tools of his own craft. You — wake the bell ringer at St Giles and tell him sound the peal for all the other church bells to ring. No citizen must sleep this night, no corner of the city be left unsearched ..."

Inside St Giles, look for the memorial to Robert Louis Stevenson writing with his quill pen, propped up in bed. The writer, Michael Morpurgo, whose favourite book is Robert Louis Stevenson's *Treasure Island,* also likes to write from the comfort of his bed. The poet Robert Fergusson — you'll

meet him again when you reach the Canongate — is commemorated too.

But perhaps the most dramatic memorial is to Robert Burns. The main west window was installed in 1985 and shows different aspects of Burns's poetry — romantic love, his love of the natural world and his belief in the equality of man. What can you decipher amongst the vivid colours of the stained glass?

Cross the High Street when you leave St Giles, and if you've the nerve, visit Mary King's Close. Rumours abound about ghosts and apparitions ... Can you imagine living in one of the hundreds of cellars — some still undiscovered — which honeycomb this area? I was most impressed by Jan-Andrew Henderson's creepy book, *Secret City*, set in the vaults under South Bridge, which brings this subterranean world to spine-chilling life.

Mary King's Close was once a bustling series of narrow streets, lined by

From *Secret City*
by Jan-Andrew Henderson:

"They called it the Underground City," said Charlie's father in a whisper. "The places where the very poorest people lived. It was a long time ago, mind you, and it's all been built over or hidden, so lots of local people think it never really existed." His father tapped the side of his nose. "But I know it does."

high tenements. In 1753, the Burgh Council decided to build the Royal Exchange on the site of what is now the City Chambers. In order to do so they blocked the entrances and knocked down a number of the tenements, using the lower floors as foundations for their grand new buildings. It is said that some people didn't leave their homes in time ...

Nearby Advocate's Close is where Lucy and Will live, Joan Lingard's present-day protagonists in her historical murder mystery, *The Sign of the Black Dagger*.

Cockburn Street curls down to your left towards Waverley Station, named after Sir Walter Scott's *Waverley* novels, the Harry Potter bestsellers of their time. Everybody who could get their hands on these thrilling historical adventures read them. Near the top of Cockburn Street, Fleshmarket Close — a cascade of stone steps — leads towards the site of the old meat market.

It was amongst these streets and closes that Nicola Morgan planned her novel:

In *Fleshmarket,* I wanted readers to smell the foulness of ancient Edinburgh. To do that, I had to be there and let my imagination combine with reality. So I wandered the tiny streets, the dark wynds, the slippery ancient cobbles of Fleshmarket Close; I went underground; I saw it in rain, sunshine, wind and snow; I sat with my notebook and a twenty-first-century cappuccino, and sent my spirit back in time. I wanted readers to feel the stinking slime, the disease, the crime, the seeping walls, the lethal cold, the dangerous towering buildings, the incredible overcrowding. The readers of *Fleshmarket* suffer — before they curl up to sleep in their cosy beds.

Nicola Morgan

From *Fleshmarket*
by Nicola Morgan:

A clanging. Clattering, shouting. One of the new fire-carts being pulled at speed by black horses came jangling round a corner, uniformed men running beside it. At the same time Robbie smelt the smoke. He held his breath to see which way they would go. Away from his home they clattered and he breathed again in relief. If you lived in the Old Town you had to fear fire even more than disease. Robbie had his own memory to fuel his fear.

Walk to the crossroads. The Tron Kirk overlooks Hunter Square, which is always especially packed during the Festival in August; full of colour and noise as

eager actors and performers from Fringe shows try to catch your eye.

History mixes easily with the present day, anything can happen ...

From *Dragonfire*
by Anne Forbes:

Lord Rothlan was stunned by the High Street! It was not the houses that drew his attention; they had not changed much over the centuries although they were considerably cleaner. No, it was the traffic and the colourful throngs of people that drew his attention. Cars and buses were unknown to him and the fact that even young children were completely unafraid of the massive monsters that growled up and down the street, amazed him ...

... From time to time he looked at the upper reaches of the tenements that line the High Street, remembering the old cry of "Gardyloo" that signalled the filthy Edinburgh habit of throwing dirty water, or worse, from the windows into the street. The church, now standing at a busy crossroads, was an outstanding landmark and walking round it into Hunter Square, he glanced upwards and saw Amgarad perched like a gargoyle on the roof.

3. From Holyrood to the Tron

From *Secrets of the Fearless*
by Elizabeth Laird:

It was a wild night, raw, with rain in the air. The bitter wind picked up a fallen pigeon's feather by the castle at the top of the hill and whirled it all the way down Edinburgh's long High Street to the palace at the bottom. It howled round the crazy jumble of chimney pots on the tops of the towering narrow houses, making the pigeons stagger on their ledges. Far down below, in the tight little wynds and closes, cats crept for shelter into doorways and under steps, fluffing out their fur.

A man and a boy, their shoulders hunched against the cold, were walking down the hill, ignoring the bursts of song and laughter erupting from the taverns. Neither of them spoke until the man cleared his throat, put a hand on the boy's shoulder and said, "The question is, John my boy, what do we do now?"

We'll start from Holyrood, and head uphill.

The Palace of Holyrood House is associated with the sad life of Mary Queen of Scots, including the dramatic murder of her secretary, Rizzio, whose blood still stains the floorboards of her apartments — or so the guides tell us. Lord Darnley, Mary's husband at the time, was suspicious of the handsome Italian courtier's influence on his wife and, along with a number of Protestant nobles, plotted David Rizzio's shocking murder; it is said that he was stabbed fifty-seven times in front of the heavily pregnant Mary. The building is well used by such writers as Mollie Hunter and Frances Mary Hendry in their historical novels. It was apparently built on the spot where King David held up a cross (a holy rood) to protect himself from the approaching antlers of an angry stag. His tactics worked — the stag disappeared into thin air.

The Palace sits in beautiful surroundings. Holyrood Park must be one of the most stunning back gardens in the world and it's provided an atmospheric backdrop for many

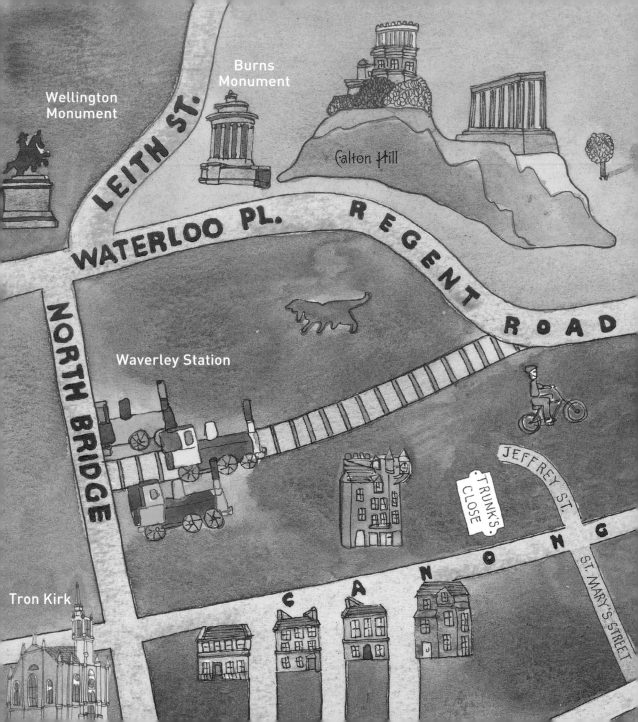

Holyrood Abbey

Abbey
Strand

Holyrood Palace

Canongate Kirk

ABBEYHILL

Scottish
Parliament

CRICHTON'S
CLOSE

QUEEN'S DR.

Salisbury Crags &
Arthur's Seat

Scottish
Poetry
Library

HOLYROOD ROAD

Dynamic Earth

stories, including recent novels by John Fardell and Anne Forbes.

From *The Flight of the Silver Turtle* by John Fardell:

Ben banked onto a curving course to bring them round Arthur's Seat on its northern side where he knew St Margaret's Loch lay. Just beyond the hill, they could see the floodlit buildings of Edinburgh's city centre.

Lower and lower they flew, rooftops slipping beneath them. They would be over Holyrood Park any minute now. Ben tried to remember everything he needed to do to bring their speed down further. Nose up slightly ... flaps down ... reduce motor speed more. He had been worried about landing at night for the whole flight. Now he was terrified. The whole park looked inky black and featureless. No sign of the loch. This was madness. They should have landed on the sea.

Anne Forbes

Not long after we were married, my husband gave me a beautiful brooch in the shape of a golden dragon. It inspired me to write a short story about Edinburgh called *Sir James and the Dragon*. Arthur's Seat, the great hill that dominates the Edinburgh skyline, was an instinctive choice of location not only for the dragon's den but as a home for the little people of the story — for often in my scrambles over its steep slopes I had thought of Arthur's Seat as a magical place. Once written, the manuscript lay undisturbed in a drawer for many years until one day I took it out and re-read it. New possibilities sprang to mind and, fired with enthusiasm, I added more characters to the story and broadened the plot. So, it is from this little tale that *Dragonfire* developed — a fantasy story set in present-day Edinburgh, featuring monsters, magicians, magic carpets and, of course, a dragon.

Joan Lingard found the seeds of her novel, *The Sign of the Black Dagger*, in the streets around Holyrood Palace.

Joan Lingard

Until the late nineteenth century debtors could be imprisoned, but they had a sanctuary, a safe place where they could escape from the law: the precincts of Holyrood Abbey and the park beyond. Spaced out across the roadway in Abbey Strand you can see three brass letters — S S S — which mark the boundary. Cross that, and you were safe. One day a week, however, the debtors could roam freely, from midnight Saturday to midnight on the Sabbath. So, late on Sunday evenings, debtors could be seen, some in carriages, others in sedan chairs, the rest walking or running, heading down the High Street, followed by messengers-at-arms dressed in their royal livery, carrying black ebony sticks tipped with silver, known as Wands of Peace, hoping to nab a debtor who had left it rather late. They only had to tap him on the shoulder — like in a game of tag — and they had him! This story had always intrigued me and led me to write *The Sign of the Black Dagger*.

From *The Sign of The Black Dagger* by Joan Lingard:

I glanced up at the Tron clock. Nine minutes to go.

... "Hurry, Papa, hurry!" urged Will.

He was doing his best. Once he skidded and would have fallen had we not held on to him. "Five minutes," said somebody behind us. We broke into a jogging-trot. By now we were in the middle of a large crowd. When we reached the foot of the Canongate, we all surged across the road together, rounding the Girth Cross, making for the Abbey Strand, which lay but a few yards away, and for safety.

I have to declare another interest, too, in this fascinating, medieval street: I was born in the heart of it, in the Canongate — in a taxi cab!

Now there's a story on which Joan has not *yet* based a novel!

The extraordinary Scottish Parliament building houses the debating chamber in which Scotland's members of parliament discuss the country's progress and future — creating new stories for the nation.

As you start to walk up the Canongate — named after the canons, or monks, of St Augustine at Holyrood Abbey — don't miss the wall of quotations from such writers as Sir Walter

27

Scott, Robert Louis Stevenson, Hugh MacDiarmid, Edwin Morgan and Robert Burns. And can you find Andrew Carnegie's name? Born and brought up in Dunfermline, he emigrated to the United States when he was twelve years old, where he made a vast fortune from steel and used much of the money to fund the building of public libraries, schools and universities there and in Scotland.

The first line of Robert Louis Stevenson's well-loved verse about the enduring power of poetry is quoted on the Canongate wall:

Bright is the ring of words
When the right man rings them,
Fair the fall of songs
When the singer sings them.
Still they are carolled and said —
On wings they are carried —
After the singer is dead
And the maker buried.

Just past Whitefoord House, look up to your right towards Calton Hill, and on Regent Road you'll see a memorial to Robert Burns. Most of the money for this memorial was raised in India and, once a marble statue of the poet was completed, the remaining funds were used to erect the monu-ment that you can see today. Some people complained that the statue was dwarfed by the monument, but in the end, because of pollution damage, it was removed for safekeeping and can now be seen in the National Portrait Gallery on Queen Street.

When you reach Crichton's Close, look up at the building on your left and read the wrought ironwork inscription, "A Nation is forged in the hearth of poetry." Then turn down Crichton's Close to find the Scottish Poetry Library, a modern building full of light. Packed with poetry books from all over the world, it is often full of school children enjoying writing workshops with such poets as Gerry Cambridge, Diana Hendry and Valerie Thornton. If you ever have a question about poetry, this is the place to come.

If you continue to walk down Crichton's Close, you will reach Holyrood Road, at the foot of which is what looks like an outsize tent. This is Our Dynamic Earth, an exciting, interactive visitor attraction which tells the story of Planet Earth, from the big bang onwards. At the foot of Crichton's Close are offices and studios from which BBC Scotland broadcasts, and on the other side of the road you will see the building in which *The*

Scotsman, one of Scotland's daily newspapers, is created. Just imagine, all those journalists in search of the elusive "exclusive" — a story that nobody has told before.

Return to the Canongate and on your right, outside the Canongate Kirk, you'll see a figure striding down the hill. Except that he never goes anywhere because this is the statue of Robert Fergusson, a poet whose short, troubled life lasted from 1750 to 1774. He died destitute, and his grave — in the Canongate Kirkyard — was unmarked until Robert Burns bought the headstone you see now.

Directly across the road is the Museum of Edinburgh in Huntly House, which is full of stories of the city going back to the time of the Roman encampment at Cramond two thousand years ago. You'll find Greyfriars Bobby's collar and bowl here.

Back on the right-hand side of the Canongate, the People's Story is housed in the Canongate Tolbooth, once a prison, and through words, pictures and photographs, tells more stories of ordinary Edinburgh people. Amongst the exhibits are pictures of the great Netherbow Port. If you had been making the same journey up the

From *Fleshmarket*
by Nicola Morgan:

The Canongate Tolbooth's turrets pierced the scudding charcoal sky above them, its tiny windows black. Next to it, sharing a wall, the new tavern, its noise swelling through the open door. Once inside the Tollbooth, he was pushed along corridors, down worn stone stairs slippery with grease and dirt.

Canongate before 1764, you would have seen it looming ahead. It was one of several gates in the walls which encircled the city, and marked the end of the Canongate. The gate-keepers would demand payment of a toll, and there were those so poor that they were never able to leave, or to gain access the city — depending on which side of the ports they were born. The Netherbow Port was demolished towards the end of the eighteenth century, but a stone carving from the original gate is mounted by the entrance to the Scottish Storytelling Centre — a purpose-built building on the right after you have crossed the road into the High Street. The old Netherbow Port Bell has been re-housed in the Storytelling Centre's tower and fittingly, even the

From *The Spanish Letters*
by Mollie Hunter:

Straddling the street here was the Netherbow Port, the easternmost gate in the city
walls, with Holyrood a few hundred yards
off and the street called the Canongate
connecting the two. If Tod and the Cleek
has passed this way, Jamie reasoned, they
would have been seen by the gatekeeper on
duty at the Netherbow and he hailed the
man with the question.

"Aye, they went through as soon as the
gates were opened at dawn," the man
shouted in reply, "the king was out early at
the hunt this morning."

bell has a story to tell! Its Latin inscription translates as:

"To God be the Glory, Michael
Burgerhuis of Middleburgh
made me at the request of the
senate and people of Edinburgh in 1621. And I was hung
on the topmost tower. Wha
Daur Meddle Wi Me?"

Judy Paterson, a storyteller and writer,
invites you inside the Scottish Storytelling Centre:

Step inside this magic place and meet
witches, wizards, giants, goblins, fair-
ies and every character you ever heard
of in a story. There is a secret bothy, a
secret garden and a magical story wall
to explore. Here Storytellers take you
into the past, into the future, around
the world and across the universe. They
look like normal people but if you think
you see a Storyteller and ask, maybe
you'll go home with a story.

How can you resist?

Judy Paterson

Detail from Julie Lacome's Mile of Stories mural

The Scottish Storytelling Centre has storytelling resources, exhibits in intriguing boxes and a programme of theatre and storytelling events throughout the year. There's a reviving café for those in need of a break and artist Julie Lacome's detailed and colourful Mile of Stories mural (see opposite) provides refreshment for the eyes too. See how many Edinburgh tales you can find — there are images from *Greyfriars Bobby, Maisie, Mary Queen of Scots, Wee Willie Winkie, Treasure Island* and many more.

At the bottom of Trunk's Close, beyond John Knox's House, are the offices of Scottish Book Trust and BRAW (Books, Reading and Writing), both of which are excellent sources of information about good books to read. The bright yellow Words on Wheels van is often to be seen taking authors out and about.

Anna Gibbons, the Director of BRAW, explains:

Anna Gibbons

We want people throughout Scotland — and elsewhere — to know about the wonderful children's books written here. We invite children to meet writers and artists in our hall in Trunk's Close, and we take the authors and illustrators out of Edinburgh, touring all over Scotland. Readers love meeting their authors as much as authors love meeting their readers. We also have a website, so that if you can't come to Scottish Book Trust's Edinburgh headquarters, you can access the information about our monthly book clubs, our author directory and our book search online.

Edinburgh was a powerful centre of publishing in the eighteenth and nineteenth centuries. Many influential books and journals made their way from these streets to readers throughout the world. The literary magazine, the *Edinburgh Review,* was first published in a house near Trunk's Close in 1802 and the *New Edinburgh Review* is still going strong today.

On the left-hand side of the High Street, look for the Museum of Childhood. Watch while your parents and grandparents go all misty-eyed at the exhibits. Founded in 1955, its exhibits were almost all from the collection of its founder, a town councillor called Patrick Murray, but when the museum opened people sent artefacts from all over the world. Look at the books, games and toys with which children played in the past. Do you have toys like these?

4. Around South Bridge

Begin this part of your tour at Blackwell's Bookshop, from which books have been sold for hundreds of years. It was originally the home of James Thin Booksellers, a family firm which was amongst the first booksellers to have a mail order department, sending books to customers all over the world.

Take time to read the opening chapters of your new books sitting next to the fish ponds in the fabulous Victorian foyer of the National Museum of Scotland on Chambers Street. The museum has been extended into a modern wing, which houses stories of the nation's geography, people and culture.

Gill Arbuthnott was inspired to write her first novel, *The Chaos Clock,* during one of many visits she has made to the museum over the years.

Gill Arbuthnott

I always loved the museum as a child, haunted it during wet school holidays. There was a sense of all the people who had owned or made or worshipped the things on display — thousands of people whose lives had somehow become part of the place.

Years later, I saw the Millennium Clock for the first time. It seemed to be absolutely bursting with stories, and this idea became one of the main themes for *The Chaos Clock;* that the museum was full to overflowing with power that had accumulated stone by sword by arrowhead over the years, and was now leaking out, destabilizing time all over Edinburgh.

I've always felt that Edinburgh has a strange relationship with "normal" time anyway. Zap someone from the sixteenth-century Royal Mile to the same place today and there would be a lot of things that would look very familiar to them. Do this during the Edinburgh Festival and no one would even notice — the streets are full of people in weird outfits all the time anyway!

Edinburgh: what a place. I sometimes wonder how anyone can live here and not tell stories!

From *The Chaos Clock*
by Gill Arbuthnott:

Around the clock, a small crowd had
already gathered as though waiting for it to
explode out of the glass roof like a firework.
As the hands reached the hour, the clock
came to life.

First, music, as though an invisible
church organ hung in the air. The monkey
began to turn her handle and all the wheels
and gears in the lowest section started to
move. Bathed in red and blue light, the
great chained figure behind her looked out
from his prison.

Abruptly, the monkey stopped and the
middle section of the clock took up the
story with bells and wind chimes and
grotesque automata bobbing and whirling;
and the great convex-mirrored pendulum,

a skeleton sitting on top of it, swung slowly,
slowly, reflecting the distorted faces of its
audience.

Deeper bells sounded now, tolling, not
chiming and a circle of figures high above
David's head began to revolve. They were so
high that he hadn't looked at them closely
before, but now he saw that they showed
people suffering, in pain and frightened. He
made out a figure swathed in barbed wire
and another with a Star of David around its
neck.

The whole clock was in motion now, the
monkey turning her handle, the donkeys
shaking the bells in their mouths, red light
glowing at the top of the spire.

The monkey stopped again, then the
music. The lights died and the whole
mechanism gradually came to rest, the last
sound the sweet notes of the wind chimes.

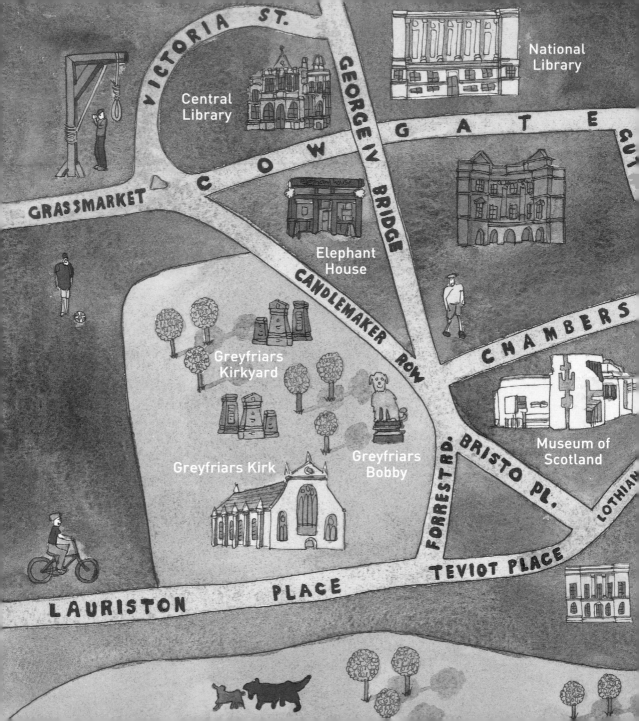

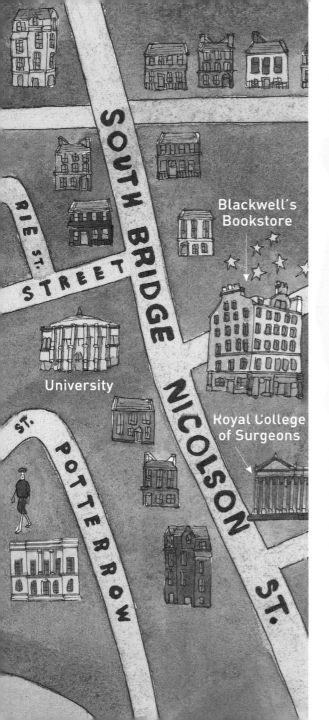

The Museum of Scotland has inspired another Edinburgh writer, John Fardell.

From *The Flight of the Silver Turtle* by John Fardell:

Zara and Ben had spent many hours in this museum ... The building was packed with so many brilliant things — stuffed animals of every description, dinosaur fossils, ancient artefacts from every part of the globe — and Zara loved it all, but it was up here, at the top of the Main Hall that had always been her favourite place in the museum. The bird's-eye view had often led her to imagine being able to fly, able to swoosh around the space and weave in and out of the pillars.

Leave the museum and head left towards George IV Bridge. On the other side of the road, there is almost always a gaggle of tourists standing with cameras pointed at a small statue of a dog.

*Greyfriars Bobby
by Sally J. Collins*

From *Greyfriars Bobby*
by Linda Strachan and Sally J. Collins:

A statue of Bobby stands proudly, close to the entrance to Greyfriars Kirkyard at the top of Candlemakers Row in Edinburgh. It watches over the path where Bobby walked every day for so many years from the kirkyard to the Coffee House.

Greyfriars churchyard

Valerie Bierman

Valerie Bierman debunks some of the mythology surrounding Greyfriars Bobby.

More sentimental words must have been written about Greyfriars Bobby than any other dog. Part truth, part fiction, umpteen books abound, as well as some fairly awful films. Jock, the Skye terrier's owner, was not a poor shepherd eking out a living in the Scottish hills, but a night-watchman employed in the city, and Bobby accompanied him on his rounds. Jock died of TB in 1858 and was buried in Greyfriars churchyard, after which Bobby refused to leave the grave despite numerous attempts by the gardener to evict him! On hearing the one o' clock gun each day (except Sunday, of course), Bobby trotted off to the nearby coffee house where his dinner awaited him, a routine he maintained for the next fourteen years. Whether this was down to devotion or hunger, we shall never know. But the story continues to inspire writers and illustrators — including Ruth Brown, Forbes Macgregor, Lavinia Derwent, Eleanor Atkinson, Linda Strachan and Sally J. Collins. And for a laugh, read Terry Deary's *Horrible Histories: Bloody Scotland* for his doggy version of the story. Then decide for yourselves!

Do you think Valerie might be a cat lover?

Linda Strachan has her own reasons for retelling the story:

Linda Strachan

As a child I always felt a special connection with the Greyfriars Bobby story and the little statue at the top of Candlemakers Row — probably because my father once had a shop there, where the Coffee House that Bobby frequented used to be.

From *Greyfriars Bobby*
by Linda Strachan and Sally J. Collins:

It was around this time that the tradition began of firing a one o' clock gun from the battlements of Edinburgh Castle. It was a daily time check for the folk of Edinburgh, but wee Bobby recognised it too, and when he heard the gun he knew it was time for his meal. He was becoming famous and the children would stand outside the kirkyard to wait for him.

"Look, there he is!" they shouted, and everyone would stop to watch as Bobby ran out of the gates and headed straight for the Coffee House.

Sally Collins, the illustrator, says: "Working on *Greyfriars Bobby* gave me a chance to capture some of the atmosphere of the Old Town with its cobble-stoned grey streets and misty sea haar."

Jan-Andrew Henderson

Greyfriars Kirkyard — named after the Franciscan monks who wore grey habits — influenced Jan-Andrew Henderson for very different reasons.

I used to live in Greyfriars Graveyard.

All right, not quite inside, but my windows overlooked it. It was like having an enormous back garden — filled with dead people. And I didn't even have to mow it.

The National Covenant was signed there (look it up). It contains what was, arguably, the world's first concentration camp. It's supposed to be haunted by the McKenzie Poltergeist. It helped inspire books as diverse as *Greyfriars Bobby*, *Frankenstein* and *Old Possum's*

Entry to the Covenanters' Prison

From *Secret City*
by Jan-Andrew Henderson:

The cemetery looked very different at night — the church seemed to be carved from squat, cold shadows and gravestones were scattered across the inky lawns like blackened stumps of teeth. Charlie switched on the torch and made his way quietly round the church until he came to the grave of Allan Ramsay, hidden in thick shadow at the bottom of the building. Hands shaking, he unwrapped the shovel, looking around to see if his actions might be detected.

Book of Practical Cats. J.K. Rowling even wrote some of the first Harry Potter novel in a restaurant facing onto it, so I'm in good company.

I've used Greyfriars in all my books. *The Ghost that Haunted Itself* is about the poltergeist. *Secret City* has a fledgling bodysnatcher as a main character. In *Hunting Charlie Wilson,* the worms in the cemetery attack the hero. It all sounds a bit macabre, I admit. If my house had overlooked an allotment, I might have ended up writing cookbooks.

It's just a bit of grass with a few headstones and a church. But, like any-where in Edinburgh, it's the accompanying legends and the stories that make it so inspiring.

I hope I've added a little to that.

Walk up Forrest Road towards Teviot Place amongst many of the buildings in which Edinburgh University students and teachers live and work. The university quarters of any city are always lively, and Valerie Bierman discovered that unconventional behaviour amongst students is nothing new.

Edinburgh University opened in 1583 when the fees were £2 a year for local students and £3 for everybody else. Several different sites were occupied until the Old College was built in 1817. At that time, the policy was to educate male students only. Or at least, that's what the powers-that-be were led to believe. Dr James Barry, who graduated in 1820, pursued a medical career, which included serving in the Crimean War. But on Barry's death, "he" was found to be a "she," thus becoming the first woman graduate of Edinburgh University! Other notable graduates — all men — were Sir Arthur Conan Doyle, Robert Louis Stevenson, who tried several courses,

Valerie Bierman

but spent more time in taverns than in studying, and J.M. Barrie, the author of *Peter Pan*. More recent well-known graduates include politicians such as Gordon Brown, Malcolm Rifkind and Robin Cook; writers Norman MacCaig, George Mackay Brown and Ian Rankin, and journalists Kirsty Wark and Sally Magnusson. Dame Stella Rimington, the former Director General of MI5, studied English there.

J.M. Barrie was born in Kirriemuir in Angus in 1860. Unlike Stevenson, he was a terribly shy young man and didn't enjoy his student years. His most famous story is about Peter Pan, a boy who didn't want to grow up. James's childhood was devastated when his older brother — his mother's favourite son — was killed in an accident. James never grew very tall — probably less than five feet — and it is thought that this was caused by the shock of his brother's death.

To the south are the Meadows, a large area of parkland, which has been popular with the people of Edinburgh since it was established in the middle of the nineteenth century. The area was originally a loch, which supplied much of Edinburgh's drinking water before the first piped sup-

ply arrived in the early seventeenth century.

Continue along Potterrow and you'll find yourself back on South Bridge, where you walk past the Royal College of Surgeons, where Nicola Morgan was first told a sobering story.

This was where I heard the gruesome story that sparked *Fleshmarket*. Visit the museum, but not if you've just had a big fried breakfast. You'll find things which will make you glad you did not live (or die) long ago. When you see the cabinet that Dr Robert Knox stands in, think of me — a newspaper photographer made me stand inside it, the skeleton looming behind me, and my hand on the jar of pickled innards ...

Whereas the shock of what she discovered in that museum triggered Nicola's historical novel, it was the tranquillity of what was Nicolsons

Nicola Morgan

From *The Chaos Clock*
by Gill Arbuthnott:

Kate found her voice. "Is this just ordinary fog?"

"No indeed," said Mr Flowerdew. "It is a fog such as no one in Edinburgh has ever seen. The Lords are trying to delay us."

Whether it was coincidence, they never knew, but as he spoke, the fog rolled back from the car for a moment and they caught a glimpse of the trees and paths of the Meadows and above them a cloud-pocked sky and the full moon.

Kate let out a gasp, heard the others exclaim.

The moon was blood red.

"What is it?" David managed to ask. "What's happened to the moon?"

"It is an eclipse — but it should not be happening now. We must hurry; they are close to breaking through."

Even as he spoke however, the fog closed in again, hiding the disfigured moon and forcing them to slow down again.

David clutched at Kate's arm. "Look!"

On one side of them, where there should have been the level grass of the Meadows, there was a rippling body of water, and on the other, so close that twigs scraped the windows of the car, the edge of a dense tract of forest.

"What's happening?"

Mr Flowerdew kept his eyes on the non-existent road as he replied, "This is what used to be here hundreds of years ago. The past is breaking loose." Around them, the fog had closed in again.

café, on the corner of South Bridge opposite the Festival Theatre, which provided the ideal writing environment for the then unknown Jo Rowling when she came to live in Edinburgh.

Head past Blackwell's towards the Tron Church on the corner of the High Street, walking across South Bridge over the Cowgate below.

From *Secret City*
by Jan-Andrew Henderson:

These tenements happened to have been built in front of a gigantic bridge but they were so tall that they made the structure behind almost invisible. This "South Bridge" was constructed in the eighteenth century so horses and carts could cross the Old Town without risking the steep slopes of the Cowgate valley. Under the massive bridge arches, hundreds of stone chambers linked by passages had been constructed — all easily accessible until the tenements had been built in front to hide them. The chambers were supposed to be used as storage vaults, but according to Charlie's dad, people had ended up living there. In fact, Edinburgh was so overcrowded that the citizens even dug tunnels into the steep sides of the Old Town ridge — and then inhabited those too ...

5. The New Town

By the mid-eighteenth century, the Nor Loch (to the north of Edinburgh's Old Town) was so insanitary and stinking that Lord Provost Drummond ordered it to be drained. Now the site of Waverley Station and Princes Street Gardens, this dramatic improvement in the area began the process which culminated in the development of Edinburgh's New Town — a haven for the wealthy from the increasing squalor of the overcrowded Old Town. The New Town with its broad, orderly streets and green spaces, was the prize-winning design of architect James Craig, and was one of the first examples of town planning.

Who better to introduce the New Town of Edinburgh than the award-winning writer Joan Lingard?

I have lived in the Georgian New Town of Edinburgh for more than thirty years and I love living here! I love its wide streets, its feeling of light, and the wonderful views you get of the Firth of Forth and Fife as you walk down Hanover or Frederick Street. I love its squares and gardens. There are gardens everywhere: Princes Street, for a start, but also

Joan Lingard

41

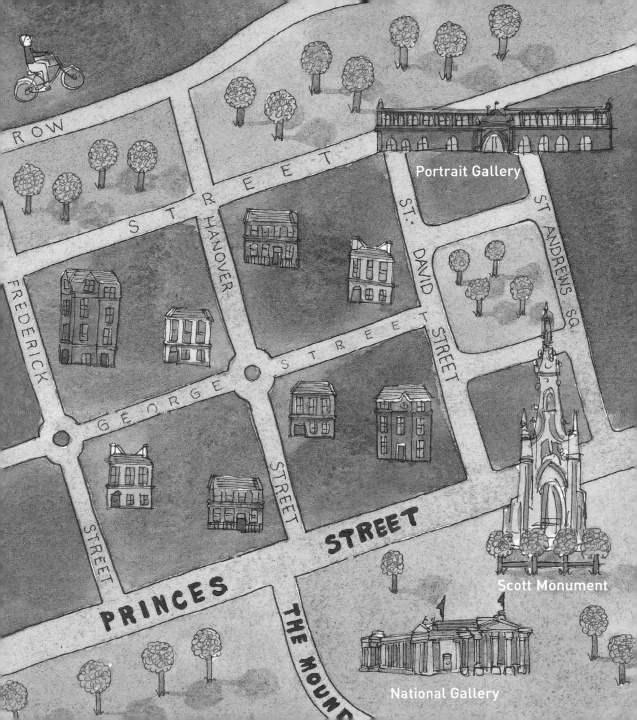

ROW

STREET

Portrait Gallery

FREDERICK

HANOVER

ST. DAVID

ST ANDREWS SQ.

STREET

GEORGE STREET

STREET

STREET

STREET

PRINCES STREET

THE MOUND

Scott Monument

National Gallery

Queen Street, Royal Circus, Moray Place, Ainslie Place, Drummond Place, with the trees making an oasis of green in amongst the buildings.

From *A Flute in Mayferry Street* by Eileen Dunlop:

Street upon street, it stretches back from the familiar Edinburgh of the picture postcards, with its sculptured green terraces in Princes Street Gardens, and great black upheaving of castle and rock, an elegantly woven web of straight, wide roads and rising, moon-shaped crescents; slate-roofed terraces of greying stone with rows of long sash-windows, spiky iron railings, wide flights of steps and shiny, important front doors. There are gardens too, set among hedges of box and hawthorn, country hedges trimmed for town, full of lime and elm and flowering currant; here and there is a house wrapped in a cloak of dusty black ivy, or a shawl of cobwebby Virginia creeper, and through gaps between the houses, unexpected, plunging vistas of cobbled street lead the eye far across the dark, piled-up roofs of the city and the silver line of the river Forth, to a hazy patchwork of farmland along the shores of Fife.

And then there is the Charlotte Square Garden where in August our huge international tented book fair takes place and is thronged by children and adults who come to hear writers talk about their work. In that same square, at Number Seven, you can find the Georgian House, furnished as it was in the early part of the nineteenth century, recreating the way Edinburghers lived then. Next door to that, at Number Six, is Bute House, the residence of our First Minister.

Few cities have as many people living in their centres as Edinburgh. This means that in the evening it doesn't become dead and deserted. There are businesses, too, which as a writer, I like, as they give variety and a feeling of different lives going on. We have art galleries — the Portrait Gallery in Queen Street among them — but also small, privately owned ones, second-hand bookshops, restaurants, cafés, pubs, hairdressers, flower shops, food shops, antique shops. Then, of course, there is Princes Street, famous all over the world, which was part of the first phase of the New Town.

By the mid-eighteenth century, the mediaeval old town was bursting at the seams and overflowing. The tenements were crowded and insanitary and people — those who could afford it

Joan Lingard

— wanted to have more space and light and air so the Nor' Loch was drained and they started to move downhill, to the north.

From *The Sign of the Black Dagger* by Joan Lingard:

Previously lawyers used to reside here and in other closes nearby but they have been moving out to go and live down in the New Town, which has wide, open streets and the houses are only three or four storeys high. This is where Maman herself would like to live ...

... "There is less stink down in the New Town," says our mother.

Thus the New Town was founded. In due course two of Scotland's most famous writers came to live here: Robert Louis Stevenson at 17 Heriot Row, and Sir Walter Scott at 39 North Castle Street.

Joan Lingard

Some people love the peace of the suburbs or the country, far from city noise and activity. For me, it is the activity of the city that stimulates me as a writer. I enjoy escaping to hills and glens, but, somehow, it is the walking of city streets that sets my imagination going. I love especially walking around the New Town at the time of day when the light is fading and the lights are coming on but people have not yet drawn their curtains. A glimpse of a lit room as one passes by is like seeing a little tableau. I don't want to be invited in and shown it in detail. I only want an impression. My imagination can do the rest. My husband says I am a nosy parker! In return, I say that, as a novelist, I am a student of human nature. A good excuse!

Charlie James, the author of the comic novel, *Fish,* is another regular visitor to Edinburgh's Book Festival.

I love this beautiful garden, home every August to the Book Festival with its tented studios, cafés, bookstalls, workshops and carnival atmosphere. It becomes my children's summer home while the buzz and excitement of new ideas and thoughts, colours, wit and learning inspires me to write, read and live.

Charlie James

The Scottish National Portrait Gallery on Queen Street opened in 1889. There you'll find portraits, statues and busts of many great Scottish writers, including Robert Burns, Sir Walter Scott, Naomi Mitchison, Edwin Morgan, Joan Lingard and Mollie Hunter. From the foyer, look up to see a pictorial history depicting hundreds of famous Scots stretching all the way round the gallery. Climb to the upper floors to see it more clearly.

Linda Strachan and Sally J. Collins chose Edinburgh as the setting for one of the Hamish McHaggis adventures:

Sally J. Collins

I painted Hamish and his friends looking up towards Edinburgh Castle through the railings along Princes Street Gardens. It is one of my favourite views and from where I marvel at the spectacular festival fireworks every year, so I feel the excitement and anticipation too! I love Princes Street Gardens, especially during the Festival when the Victorian carousel is in full flight beside the fabulous golden fountain.

I have travelled on Edinburgh's big red tour bus several times, so it was fun to include it as part of Hamish's Edinburgh adventure and to add in the controversial new Parliament building, too.

Linda Strachan

At the foot of the Mound where Hamish and his friends fix the Whirry Bang's broken wheel are the huge stone columns of the National Gallery of Scotland, which are set on steps that look like they were made for giants — very appropriate for small characters.

From "Embra Buses" by Stephanie Green (from *The Thing That Mattered Most: Scottish Poems for Children*):

You can see the hale world fae the tap
of a bus:
turbans and burkas, saris wi cardis,
Kilts wi Doc Martens,
spiky-haired Goths,
Hoodies and Neds in Burberry caps,
Morningside ladies in sensible hats.

Journeys begin and end in Waverley Station. In her book, *Remembrance*, Theresa Breslin wrote of a journey that a young boy began there during World War I; a boy who was determined to play his part in the conflict.

From *Remembrance*
by Theresa Breslin:

Alex left the lorry at its first delivery
on the outskirts of the city. Although
it meant more walking for him, he
considered it too risky to wait on. He
had all his maps with him and followed
Maggie and Charlotte's bus route to
Waverley Station. After buying his ticket
he went to find his train. He made a point
of asking the guard, the engine driver,
and two different people on the platform
if this was the London train. He decided
not to take a seat. Better to keep moving
about the train. That way no-one would
be sure where he had actually got off.
They were rattling along the long viaduct
at Berwick before the guard inspected his
ticket ...

... The guard winked at him. "Going to
enlist, son? Better grow a moustache or
you'll never get away with it."

In *A Sound of Chariots*, Bridie, moving
on after her father's premature death,
arrives at Waverley Station.

From *A Sound of Chariots*
by Mollie Hunter:

The train pulled into Waverley
Station and she got out into the black
bustle of it clutching tightly on to her
suitcase with one hand and on to the
purse in her pocket with the other for
her mother had warned her well about
pick pockets. Clumsily dodging
through all the hazards of the busy
station, she made for the entrance.
The thronging pavements, the noise,
the sensation of being hemmed
threateningly in by all the tall buildings,
held her dazed for a moment. A woman
barged into her and stepped back,
glaring.

"I'm terribly sorry — I wasn't lo—" she
began to apologize, but the woman only
looked her up and down contemptuously
and hurried on, muttering under her
breath

"It won't be like the village, remember,"
her mother had warned her. "They're in
too much of a hurry for good manners in
the city."

Statue of Sir Walter Scott at the foot of the Scott Monument

Dominating the east end of Princes Street Gardens is the Scott Monument. After Sir Walter Scott died in 1832, a competition was launched to design a fitting memorial to a man who had done so much for the city and the country. The winner was George Meikle Kemp, but he never saw the finished building because he fell into the Union Canal and drowned two years before it was completed. The Scott Monument is just over sixty-one metres tall, and required foundations to be dug nearly sixteen metres below ground. The marble statue of Sir Walter with his devoted dog, Maida, at his feet was carved from a single block of Italian marble by Sir John Steell. A bronze copy sits in Central Park in New York alongside a sculpture of Robert Burns, also by Steell.

In some ways, Sir Walter Scott was a one-man tourist board for Scotland. His novels introduced the country and its people to readers throughout the world, and in 1822 he organized a visit from King George IV. Scott persuaded the king to wear a kilt, and insisted that everybody who came to any of the parties and balls organized during the visit also wore Highland dress, which wasn't the custom at the time. Unhappy about baring his knees in public, the king wore pink tights — a fashion disaster which, fortunately, was not adopted by the Scots.

Scott was careless with money, and when he found himself in terrible debt he decided to write his way out of trouble. Gradually, he began to pay off his debts, but his health suffered badly from the relentless task of writing and he died in 1832. It is ironic that a man who couldn't look after his money now looks out from the Bank of Scotland's five pound notes!

Nicola Morgan

Jamie Jauncey

Nicola Morgan has a bone to pick about King George IV's visit.

I lived in Dalkeith when I was writing *Fleshmarket*. I discovered that when George IV came to Edinburgh, he stayed in Dalkeith (because Edinburgh stank) and the journey that used to take me at least twenty minutes, along the Old Dalkeith Road, he actually did in ... nineteen minutes. Call that progress?

The writer Jamie Jauncey recalls growing up in the New Town:

It seems extraordinary now that when I was growing up in the New Town, a few hundred yards from Robert Louis Stevenson's childhood home at 17 Heriot Row, little had changed since he'd been a boy, a century before. The streets I knew in the 1950s were still cobbled and gas lamps hissed above the pavements. A woman with a barrel-organ drawn by a Shetland pony turned her handle for pennies under our tall windows. Sometimes a one-man-band came by with a bass drum on his back, a squeezebox on his front and cymbals between his knees. Rag-and-bone men clopped past on their carts. The fishwives came up from Newhaven with their striped petticoats and heavy

From *Fleshmarket* by Nicola Morgan:

Everything, every detail, was organized by the famous writer, Walter Scott. Robbie remembered his father explaining that the visit had been Mr Scott's idea in the first place. "It is the first time for two hundred years that a British king has come to Edinburgh," said his father proudly as they watched the preparations ... "We live in a new Scotland, Robbie, and Edinburgh is at the forefront."

... Dozens of carts dragged sand from Portobello beach and spread it on the cobbles. Mr Scott's orders, said Robbie's father, to muffle the sounds of horses and allow the bands to be heard. Each day the Town Criers announced new orders from the great man. Residents to empty their chamber pots and buckets every morning into the public drains, not the cobbles below. Privies, where they existed, to be emptied too, not left until they overflowed. Every window facing a street to have a light shining in it after dark.

creels, then the Ingan Johnny would appear in his beret, wheeling his bicycle, the handlebars draped with strings of onions. When the wind blew from the south the thick smell of malt and hops drifted up from the city's breweries, as it had done for more than a century. But when it came from the east, along Heriot Row, it seemed to carry with it Robert Louis Stevenson's love of stories, and as it rattled at our windows I longed for the tales our colourful cast of visitors had to tell.

Valerie Bierman enjoys Robert Louis Stevenson's poetry in *A Child's Garden of Verses,* which recalls a rather solitary childhood in and around Edinburgh, including the nightly ritual of the lamplighter.

First published in 1896, some verses now seem rather sentimental, but Stevenson wrote of activities enjoyed by all children — playing in the stream, flying high on a swing or reading under the covers at night. He was a sickly child, and spent long spells convalescing but his nurse Alison Cunningham fed his imagination with blood-thirsty bible stories and tales of Scottish history. He played games in the gardens of his homes in Howard Place in Inverleith and latterly Heriot Row, from the windows of which he loved to watch the lamplighter igniting the gas street lights every evening. His

other favourite haunts were the family's rented cottage in Swanston in the Pentlands and his grandfather's manse at Colinton. Many of his poems reflect his delight at country living inventing not only games, but as an only child, playmates too.

A verse from "The Lamplighter" is inscribed on a plaque on the railings of 17 Heriot Row:

For we are very lucky, with a
lamp before the door,
And Leerie stops to light it as
he lights so many more;
And O! before you hurry by
with ladder and with light,
O Leerie, see a little child and
nod to him to-night!

Robert Louis Stevenson, from
A Child's Garden of Verses

There's a small stone erected to Robert Louis Stevenson in West Princes Street Gardens, with the most simple of inscriptions carved by the poet and artist, Ian Hamilton Finlay: "A man of letters R.L.S. 1850–1894."

Another man of letters was Kenneth Grahame, the writer of one of the most famous children's classics, *The Wind in the Willows.* Grahame was born at 32

Valerie Bierman

Castle Street on March 8th, 1859, but his connection with the city was brief as his family moved to the Highlands the following year, and most of Grahame's adult life was spent in England.

In Picardy Place stands a statue of Sherlock Holmes, one of the first of many literary detectives. He was the creation of Sir Arthur Conan Doyle who spent his early childhood in a house nearby. Sir Arthur was a doctor, but took the opportunity to write detective novels when business was slow.

Alexander McCall Smith, Professor of Medical Law at the University of Edinburgh, and a writer for children and adults, has set a series of adult stories, serialized daily in the *Scotsman,* in and around Scotland Street.

Alexander McCall Smith

I like the New Town of Edinburgh, with its handsome, wide streets. Scotland Street is one of these streets, and it has a secret. Well, it's not a very well-kept secret, because quite a few people know about it, but there's an old railway tunnel that runs underneath it and goes all the way under the city up as far as Waverley Station. If you go to the end of Scotland Street you will see the entrance to this tunnel — a great, gaping black cave. This entrance is barred, but I was taken in there once and walked quite a way up, under dripping stalactites. It was very atmospheric!

Nicola Morgan, though, can't help being drawn from the New back to the Old Town.

Nicola Morgan

One experience sums up my feelings about Edinburgh old and new, and my memories of writing *Fleshmarket*. You can have this experience too: take a top-deck bus journey along Princes Street, preferably in sunshine, though sheeting rain works too. Your view towards the Old Town is, for me, the most wonderful cityscape in the world — a pulsing crowd of higgledy houses, stacked, ready to topple, like spectators craning their necks to see into the New Town. The foulness may have gone but the Old Town remains a powerful force.

6. Stockbridge

Diana Hendry & Hamish Whyte

Writer Diana Hendry and writer and publisher Hamish Whyte have chosen to make their home in Stockbridge.

Stockbridge has kept its busy, village feel. On the north edge of the New Town, near the Royal Botanic Gardens, it's named after the bridge built for cattle in 1785 over the Water of Leith. Slightly "bohemian," once known for antique shops, it now has lots of charity shops. It also has a long association with writers and artists.

The painter, Henry Raeburn (1756–1823), famous for his "Skating Minister," was born and lived in Stockbridge. James Hogg (1770–1835), author of *Confessions of a Justified Sinner*, lodged in Deanhaugh Street in 1813. A plaque at 21 Comely Bank tells us the historian and essayist, Thomas Carlyle (1795–1881), who was a very witty letter writer, lived there for two years after his marriage to Jane Welsh (1801–66) in 1826.

Robert Michael Ballantyne (1825–94), author of *The Coral Island* (1858) and other adventure stories, was born at 25 Ann Street (now one of the most expensive streets of Georgian houses in the city), and attended Edinburgh Academy before joining the Hudson's Bay Company in Canada. He based *The Young Fur-Traders* (1856) on his experiences there. Robert Louis Stevenson, a later pupil at the Academy, was a fan and there's a story that as a teenager he met Ballantyne in the street and invited him to dinner but Ballantyne couldn't come — what an interesting meeting that would have been!

From *Fleshmarket*
by Nicola Morgan:

How could he live in a house like this, with its own door, and big windows gulping in sunlight? And no filth on the street. A wide street with air flowing through it. Saxe-Coburg Place, it was called, which spoke to him of royalty and foreign courts.

... Looking through the railings to the side, he could see into the nearest room on the ground floor. Try as he might, he could not stop his eyes opening wide. It was huge! The ceilings high, the plaster flowing in teardrops around the corners. An enormous fireplace, surrounded by a white carved frame, much wider than the fireplace itself, a ledge above it. The clean straight lines perfect.

Diana Hendry lives in the interesting group of houses built in the nineteenth century for artisans (masons, black-smiths etc.) known as the Colonies. Many of the streets have trades insignia on the end wall. One of her novels, *You Can't Kiss it Better,* uses local settings.

I began writing *You Can't Kiss It Better* soon after I moved to Edinburgh and found a flat in Stockbridge Colonies. I wanted to write about the feeling of not belonging — which was how I felt at the time — and also about the river, the Water of Leith. The river reminded me of Kenneth Grahame's *The Wind in the Willows.* (Kenneth Grahame was born in Edinburgh.) My story is about four children in foster care.

The story's mainly told by Anna and if you go down the metal steps by Pizza Express you will find yourself walking along the Water of Leith as Anna does on her way home from school. Carry on and you'll see a tall house with balconies. Anna lives here with Brent, Raymond and Sam — four children with a lot of problems. (Sam, like Mole in *The Wind in the Willows,* is very homesick.) Following the river towards Leith, you come to a spooky part, dark with trees, shrubs and broken grave-stones. This is where Anna sees the mysterious River Woman. Towards the end of the story there's a terrible flood — as there was in reality in Spring 2000.

The Water of Leith Walkway will — with a few kinks and detours — lead you by the river north to Leith, or south to Balerno at the foot of the Pentlands, where it ends at the High School.

From *You Can't Kiss it Better*
by Diana Hendry:

Yesterday I came back from school along the river.

... All along the wall at the far side of the river there are holes where the pigeons live. Like apartments. Like a housing estate for pigeons. If they had numbers it would go, No.1 Pigeon Avenue and so on.

I haven't seen any rats or moles by the river, like in the book. Though I did see a toad. My favourite character in WITW is Mole. I like it when Mole is out with Ratty and he smells his home and suddenly this great homesick longing comes over him and he thinks his heart will break. And he knows it's a shabby dingy little place and not grand like Toad Hall, but it's home and he loves it.

Another extract from the same book offers a different perspective on the Water of Leith.

From *You Can't Kiss it Better* by Diana Hendry:

MY RIVER by Raymond Eccles, Form 6N

The name of my river is the Water of Leith which is a very funny name for a river. Other rivers are called rivers, like the River Thames (in London) or the River Mersey (in Liverpool). I like the name of my river because it has a nice sound.

If you look at the river on a map, it is like a long riggling green snake running through the city. Of course it is not really green. It is all colours of grey and brown. More browns than in a paint box.

The river is 35km long. It starts in the Pentland hills and goes out into the sea at the port of Leith. Maybe it should be called The Water of the Pentland Hills.

. . . What I like most about the river is that it is very changeful. Sometimes it is slow and quiet like an old dog you can pat. And other days it is wild and feerce and could brake down walls and maybe even houses.

But the river is always there.

In order to write, the author Charlie James takes herself away from the hustle and bustle for some peace and quiet, and inspiring views.

Charlie James

I work from a magic room right at the top of a New Town house. Each morning I climb 96 stairs, open a white-panelled door with its brass door knob and settle into my writing room, with its views over the city. I look down on the roof tops, chimneys and narrow alleys. I see the sky, the birds and the Firth of Forth. To the left is the metallic mass of Murrayfield Stadium; straight ahead the ominous, brooding spires of Fettes College, the beautiful trees of the Botanic Gardens and, on a clear day, the distant hills of the Kingdom of Fife, filling the horizon to the left. And tucked beneath the Forth Rail Bridge is Deep Sea World, a favourite haunt and a useful source of inspiration for my novel, *Fish* ...

Mike Nicholson's first novel, *Catscape,* was directly inspired by his Stockbridge surroundings.

Mike Nicholson

Catscape would never have existed without Comely Bank and Stockbridge. I wanted to enter a writing competition and, needing inspiration, I saw three different lost cat posters around Comely Bank. My mind whirred — what if lots more cats were missing? Where might they be? Who might have noticed? It seemed natural for the plot to develop in the area. Soon I had a hero who lived in Comely Bank Avenue, where the main characters also first met, and an incident in Inverleith Park, and then I blended fact and fiction, creating vaults below fictitious shops in Raeburn Place. These were inspired by a plan drawing I once saw of the vaulted archways below South Bridge. I transferred the idea to Stockbridge and invented local history to develop the plot.

Catscape was actually written in the area too, either where I lived at the time in South Learmonth Gardens or in a range of cafés nearby. So the area not only gave me the initial idea but also a setting for my story and a place for me to sit and write it in.

From *Catscape*
by Mike Nicholson:

The Edinburgh summer night was clear and, with a full moon, it seemed more dark blue than black. In only a few minutes they were at the bottom of Comely Bank Avenue, had set their bikes up as planned and were crouched down as if involved in some essential bike maintenance. The road was quiet and with the plan starting so well, both boys were more excited than nervous. Even Jock seemed to have captured the mood, sniffing the air and pricking his ears up to be alert for any new sound.

In no time they were using the crowbar to begin lifting the manhole cover.

Joan Lingard has a particular affection for the Stockbridge street that gave her the idea for one of her best-selling novels.

Three minutes walk from where I live is St Stephen Street, a lively narrow street that I have used as a setting in a number of my novels, for both children and adults. Here there are restaurants, pubs, hairdressers, beauticians, a dancing school and shops selling all manner of second-hand things from jewellery to clocks to clothes. People live here, too. It was a second-hand clothes shop that set me writing *Rags and Riches*. I started to wonder how one could make a living selling second-hand clothes. Then I imagined a shop in a basement and the owner — a woman called Isabella who has two children, a son and a daughter called Sam and Seb ... I went home and started to write.

From *Rags and Riches*
by Joan Lingard:

She keeps a second-hand clothes shop in a street that's full of shops selling second-hand things, from books to old fenders and clocks to medals and feather boas (though they're scarce) and silk petticoats (usually full of snags and runs) and woollens (usually matted). There are also two or three bars in the street, and some cafes. We like it, Seb and I. There's always something going on.

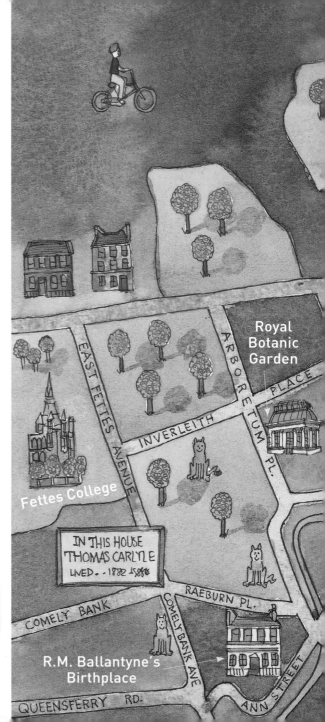

Royal
Botanic
Garden

ARBORETUM PL.

PLACE

EAST FETTES AVENUE

INVERLEITH

Fettes College

IN THIS HOUSE
THOMAS CARLYLE
LIVED . - 1882

RAEBURN PL.

COMELY BANK

COMELY BANK AVE

ANN STREET

R.M. Ballantyne's
Birthplace

QUEENSFERRY RD.

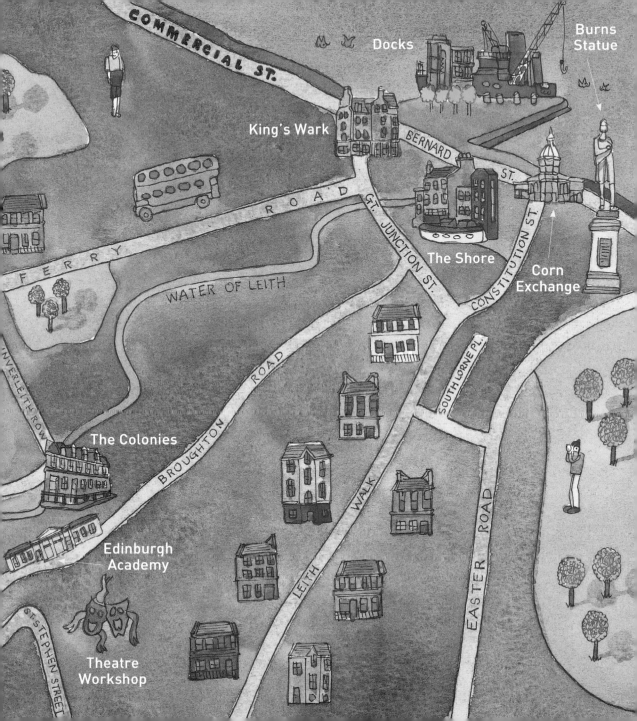

7. The Port of Leith

Elizabeth Laird spends much of her time in Edinburgh where she lives near the Grassmarket. But it was Leith — on the the shores of the Firth of Forth to the north of the city — that she visited in order to research a particularly dramatic scene in the early part of her novel, *Secrets of the Fearless*.

The Leith I first knew, forty years ago, was very different from the bright, prosperous town of today, with its sparkling new buildings and smart restaurants. Then, the streets were drab and dimly lit, and the pubs were noisy places, full of sailors from the fleets of the northern seas making the most of their shore leave.

When I was writing *Secrets of the Fearless* I prowled round Leith again, and tried to recapture the spirit of the place as it must have been two centuries ago. I had to block out the modern town: the cars, the canned music and the smart new flats on the waterfront. I sat for a long time on a bollard on the Shore, half shut my eyes, and reeled my imagination back to the great age of sail and the long war that Britain fought against Napoleon.

Behind me was a pub, the King's Wark; a place of great antiquity. It wasn't hard to see how it must have been two hundred years ago: a simple tavern with one bare-walled room lit only by tallow candles, a fire burning in the grate and the shuffle of sea-boots on sanded floorboards. It would have been crowded with men of the sea, coming off fishing boats, brigs and naval frigates, while the great three-masted fighting ships, with their triple tiers of guns and their towering structures of spars and rigging, rode at anchor out in the Forth.

Other sensations from long ago crowded in: the rumble of iron-bound cartwheels on stone-paved roads, the stench of close-packed, tumbledown houses, the darkness of unlit corners and narrow, winding streets, and for the unwary, the ever present danger of cut throats and footpads, and, perhaps even more frightening, the press-gang, lying in wait to entrap men and boys into service in the King's navy.

The fire still burns in the King's Wark, and the barman still serves brandy and wine from France as well

as good Scottish beer. But the people who crowd into the place are not sailors, but tourists from the far ends of the world. The risks are different too. You won't be snatched by the press-gang to fight in foreign wars. You're much more likely to be run over by an expensive car driven by one of Leith's smart new residents.

But the sea is always the sea. In those days, too, the waves lapped against the stone walls of the quays, the gulls cried mournfully overhead, and the salt tang of seaweed filled the air. The grey waters of the Forth surged backwards and forwards on the tides then as they do now, and the clouds drifted over the coast of Fife beyond them.

Leith officially became part of the city of Edinburgh in 1920. The locals voted five to one against the decision, but they were over-ruled. Local industries have included sawmills, rope makers and flour mills, and Leith was an important port for the fishing and whaling industry. The first steamship to cross the Atlantic sailed from her shores and millions of bottles of whisky have been exported on ships over the years. Cargo ships continue to arrive from all over the world and occasionally, one of the vast cruise ships which tour the world's oceans ties up at the pier next to Ocean Terminal, dwarfing the *Britannia* on which the Royal Family used to travel.

From *Secrets of the Fearless*
by Elizabeth Laird:

Half an hour later, John and his father were trudging down the quay in the port of Leith. The wind, which had fallen now, had whipped the clouds away, and a half-moon shone. It lit up the ripples on the water in the harbour and glanced off the wet cobblestones.

A couple of men, no more than dark shapes against the indigo sky, were lounging against a bollard. They murmured a polite "Good evening to you," but John was aware of their eyes on his back as he hurried after his father.

"No one could be looking for us here yet, could they?" he whispered to Patrick. He was thinking uneasily of the horseman who had passed them on the road.

Patrick didn't answer. He was scanning the ships moored alongside the quay.

"Is it that one, the boat to London?" asked John.

From *The Dark Shadow*
by Mary Rhind:

The next day their uncle, the merchant, hired a horse and cart to take them down to the Haven of Leith where his ship was waiting. Edinburgh was busy, for the first General Assembly of the new Universal Kirk, as they called the New Faith, was in progress and large crowds were thronging into the town looking for fun and excitement, many for trouble. John Knox was also in town and had been preaching against the total destruction of church buildings. In vain it seemed he was trying to curb the enthusiasm of the mobs for burning churches. They would need the buildings for their new Universal Kirk, he reasoned. It was only the statues and monuments of idolatry that were to be destroyed.

It was afternoon by the time Davie and Lizzie reached Leith with their uncle. Mr Cunningham pointed out a large vessel at the quayside. It was painted in a soft red colour and had the name Golden Lily written in gold letters across its bows, above which the painted figure of a lady rose with carved streaming hair holding a golden lily in her hand ...

"This is my ship, my children," declared the merchant proudly. "I bought her from the English."

At the junction between Bernard Street and Constitution Street stands a bronze statue of Robert Burns erected in 1898 by the Leith Burns Club.

Robert Burns was born in Galloway on January 25, 1759. He first published his poems in order to raise enough money to emigrate to Jamaica, but that book earned more than he had expected so Burns decided to move to Edinburgh in order to publish more of his work. Burns' poetry is known and loved throughout the world and his birthday celebrated everywhere with traditional Burns Suppers of cock-a-leekie soup, and haggis, neeps and tatties, a rousing rendition of Burns' epic "Tam o Shanter" as well as the traditional Immortal Memory and Toast to the Lassies.

And while you're in the vicinity of the statue of Robert Burns, look up at the frieze along the western wall of the newly refurbished Corn Exchange, which tells the story of wheat being harvested and ground into flour, before being loaded onto ships for export — all done by a cheerful group of chubby cherubs.

8. Morningside and Bruntsfield

Vivian French

The areas of Bruntsfield and Morningside are on the south-west side of the city, across the green spaces of the Meadows and Bruntsfield Links. Vivian French writes stories, plays and poems in her top floor flat in Morningside.

I love living in Morningside. If I come out of my flat and turn left it's only a ten minute walk before I'm watching the birds on Blackford Pond. I like the coots best; they're wonderfully bossy, and if any ducks come near they zoom towards them swearing dreadfully. (It's probably a good thing I don't understand Coot.) Walking round the pond or, if I'm feeling more energetic, striding up Blackford Hill, is a great way to clear my brain when I'm stuck in the middle of a tricky plot. Sometimes I have to dash home quickly before I forget a (hopefully) good idea; I've never got into the habit of carrying a notebook. I'm pretty certain that if I did I'd never have any ideas at all.

If I turn right I can be walking across the Meadows in ten minutes, along with the wild cyclists and the doggy walkers who come out whatever the weather.

Well — I *can* do it in ten minutes, but I usually get sidetracked by the charity shops. Or I bump into a friend, and we pop into Café Grande in Bruntsfield for a coffee and a chat about how hard we ought to be working. There are a lot of us writing and illustrating types living in the area; it's another bonus. Oh, and there's the fabulous Morningside Library — what would I do without it? I pop in meaning to stay for five minutes, and three hours later I'm still reading the latest teenage fiction.

Once I've crossed the Meadows I usually end up in the Museum of Scotland (especially now I'm working on a book about Egyptians, and need to check my facts). It's one of my favourite places in Edinburgh. I find something amazing every time I go.

If I'm at home I spend far too much time staring out of my front window; the bus stop is across the road, and people wait in so many different ways. There are the watch checkers ("Tchah! Isn't it here *yet?*"), the anxious ones who keep leaping into the road to see if the bus is in sight, the couldn't-care-less students, and the ladies who are so deep in conversation they almost forget to get on even when the bus does come.

My workroom is at the back of my flat, and I can see drying greens, and

The Meadows

Union Canal

Lothian Road

Melville Drive

Marchmont Crescent

Marchmont Road

The Links

Bruntsfield Place

Café Grande

Newbattle Terrace

Dominion Cinema

Morningside Library

23

Morningside Road

Cluny Gardens

Blackford Pond

Blackford Hill

back gardens, and Blackford Hill. This year two magpies nested at the top of the tree nearest my window, and they distracted me for weeks. They argued about every single stick that went into the nest *("What??? You think that will fit? You must be joking!!!)* until I began to wonder if they'd ever be finished in time to lay a single egg.

Ever since I've been thinking about a bird story ... so watch this space. *The Magpies of Morningside?*

Who knows ...

Aileen Paterson brought her young family to live in Morningside.

I've written and illustrated lots of stories about Maisie, a Scottish kitten who lives in Edinburgh. My first-ever book was *Maisie Comes to Morningside* (published in 1984) and Morningside appears in many of the others. I'd been asked by a fellow teacher and aspiring publisher to try writing a book about "something Scottish" for children. Until then I'd written nothing apart from letters and school reports, but I agreed, with all the blithe confidence of someone who hasn't a clue. One thing I did know was that I wanted nothing to do with battles in the heather, dead Queens or Loch Ness Monsters.

Although writing turned out to be a lot more difficult than I'd imagined, I knew what I wanted to write about. Ordinary present-day Scotland. I wanted to set my story in Morningside, where I lived. I wanted to draw the real tenements, my stair, the shops, the Library, the School, the Dominion Cinema and the Number 23 bus. Morningside may be far from the historic Old Town and the beautiful New Town, but it is just as rich a

Aileen Paterson

From *Maisie Comes to Morningside* by Aileen Paterson:

Over the next few days, Maisie explored Morningside with Archie, Flora and little Effie. They stood on tiptoes on the railway bridge and watched trains pass underneath — and Archie got some new numbers for his collection; they pressed their noses against shop windows and gazed longingly at toys, or sweets, or pretty ornaments — even at customers in a hairdressers, until they were chased away; they made their way to Blackford Pond, where they fed the ducks, before scrambling Blackford Hill to sit and munch contentedly at their picnic, gazing down on the rooftops of Morningside.

treasure trove for a writer, and so very Edinburgh!

In that first book I tell about Maisie's reactions when she comes to live with her granny in a flat in the genteel suburb. She is *not* a happy kitten. Until then she'd lived a life of hen-chasing, bath-dodging freedom in the Northern hills. Her dislike of the busy city traffic, her scary encounter with the posh, pernickety bossy boots, Mrs McKitty, and her gradual discovery of Morningside's charms are based on things which happened to my children. After years in the country, we moved to a Morningside flat. Three children, three cats and me. We all took a while to get used to it ...

From Maisie and the Monster *by Aileen Paterson*

From Maisie Goes to Hospital *by Aileen Paterson*

From *Maisie Comes to Morningside* by Aileen Paterson:

When they arrived at Granny's street, Maisie jumped out of the taxi and groaned to herself.

"So this is Morningside," she thought. "What a disappointment!"

Granny lived in a flat, up a stair, in one of the tall, grey tenement buildings. She did not even have a garden. Maisie's tail drooped sadly. They went upstairs and Granny made some hot cocoa. She examined the holes in Maisie's jersey and poked at the tuggy bits in her fluffy coat.

"Dearie me, Maisie Mackenzie, you look a right ticket!" she exclaimed. "You can't walk about Morningside looking like that. I'll run you a nice hot bath and give your clothes a wee wash and a mend."

Aileen Paterson

Once I got going with the story, memories and ideas rushed into my head and I began to have fun. I changed all the people into cats. Cats who wore clothes, had Scottish accents and dined on stovies and chocolate éclairs! I decided to poke gentle fun at some of the ladies who lived beside us. I turned them all into one Mrs McKitty. These ladies all wore hats from Jenners, and were afraid of nothing and no one. And of course they all had the famous Morningside "Panloaf Accent"! We got a fair few tellings-off from them. One lady, who was terribly proud of having a Bay Window and relatives who lived in very grand Ravelston Dykes, chased my children for "performing hendstends" on the precious back green. Another gave me a roasting for failing to keep the stair spotless. I hadn't noticed an ancient card, which had been hung from my front doorknob. It read: IT IS YOUR TURN TO SWEEP AND WASH THE COMMON STAIR AND BACK PASSAGE ...(!) They all told us, "You cent keep cets in a flet!" I was often highly tickled, but I felt that I might as well have moved to Timbuktu!

After a few months, the ladies had us trained and we began to explore. My daughter joined the library and my sons discovered an old coal yard nearby. Great for games and adventures. And oily tarry clothes. I was invited in for tea and home baking and my hostess asked, "Can I press you to a macaroon?" The cats took over the back green.

Like Maisie, we came to love Morningside.

Before Maisie came to Morningside, the area's most famous literary resident was Miss Jean Brodie. The charismatic schoolteacher, who famously referred to her pupils as the "crème de la crème" and herself as being in her "prime," was created by Dame Muriel Spark, who grew up in Bruntsfield in the 1930s and attended what was then James Gillespie's High School for Girls. *The Prime of Miss Jean Brodie* isn't a children's book, but it's one that many teenagers enjoy reading, as they follow the fortunes of the girls chosen to be the "Brodie set." Gill Arbuthnott, who also lives in Bruntsfield and attended James Gillespie's — many years after Muriel Spark! — says: "I had a teacher at primary school who I am still convinced modelled herself on Jean Brodie. She was one of those fabulous eccentrics who don't seem to go into teaching nowadays."

Bruntsfield Links is a favourite haunt of the illustrator, Julie Lacome.

Julie Lacome

I'm inspired by Edinburgh and especially the area of Bruntsfield where I live, with its fascinating shops, and even more fascinating shoppers. I try to make my illustrations as colourful and bustling as Bruntsfield itself. And using torn-paper collage helps, I think, to give my work a kind of 3-D effect. My favourite pastime is people (and dog!) watching and daily walks around the Bruntsfield Meadows with my cocker spaniel, Poppy, allowed me to indulge my passion all year round. There's always something going on — football, cricket, sledging, cycling, skateboarding, kite flying, juggling — that I can capture and use in my pictures and Poppy is a magnet for children and other dogs. I was very sad when Poppy died recently, but she's been immortalized in the Mile of Stories mural that I was commissioned to paint for the new Scottish Storytelling Centre in the High Street. See if you can find her, next time you visit.

Robert Dodds, who wrote *The Midnight Clowns* — a spine-chilling thriller about a two children desperately trying to escape from the kind of entertainers you definitely wouldn't want at your birthday party — found that Morningside affected his writing in a rather unusual way.

Robert Dodds

I lived for seventeen years in Morningside, a very calm and respectable suburb of Edinburgh. There are streets of calm, respectable houses with tidy gardens and polite people cutting their hedges and washing their cars. Every morning and afternoon, neat respectable children walk along the streets to and from their calm, respectable schools.

But whenever there was a dark night with no moon, I could hear troupes of supernatural clowns cackling and somersaulting out on those very same streets, rattling the doors of the neat respectable houses and trying to get in.

Now I've left Morningside. It's too scary.

Nicola Morgan also lives nearby, and loves the variety within this area of the city.

Nicola Morgan

Bruntsfield is one of my favourite areas, partly because it means I'm nearly home; partly because of the good coffee shops. Traditionally, Edinburgh authors are supposed to use coffee shops to write best-selling novels in. I have so far not managed to do this. Probably because I talk too much.

When I walk along the Union Canal, I think of Burke and Hare, who were two of the men who worked on it. Maybe that's why they didn't actually do any grave-robbing, choosing murder instead — they'd done enough digging. Once you've dug one hole, you've dug them all ...

Be careful when you walk on Lothian Road, since it's not the most attractive walk and I do it quite often, I tend to spend it looking at people and using them as inspiration for the characters in whatever book I'm writing. Most of my villains have walked along Lothian Road ...

From Lothian Road you can return to the Old Town through the Grassmarket, which used to be a grassy cattle market outside the city walls. A steep street, the West Port, once the site of one of the great city gates which feature in many historical novels, leads you towards Victoria Street.

As you walk towards Victoria Street you'll pass through West Bow with its impossibly high tenement buildings. In Honor Arundel's novel, *High House*, Emma, recently orphaned, came to live in just such a house with her bohemian aunt. It was quite a shock to her system. And ultimately this fascinating street brings you full circle — back to the High Street and Edinburgh's Old Town, where we started.

From *The Lothian Run*
by Mollie Hunter:

... Leftward down the West Bow the procession swung, and was forced to move more slowly by the narrower, twisting way. Yells, and the crash of axes on wood echoed back to them from farther ahead, and thinking of St Clair's call for a rope, Sandy shouted to Gilmour,

"They must be breaking into the rope-chandler's shop down there!"

Twenty yards from the street's junction with the Grassmarket they came on the rope-chandler's door swinging wide, and saw St Clair framed in it triumphantly displaying a coil of rope to the vanguard of the mob swirling round him. On one side of him stood the redhead Lumsden with his drum and on his other side was the shopkeeper, broadly grinning as he held one hand aloft to show the glint of a golden guinea held between thumb and forefinger.

9. A Gathering of Writers

John Fardell:

Edinburgh fires my imagination. How could you walk though the city centre when the haar is rolling up from the Forth and not want to write a children's adventure story?

I keep most of the Edinburgh geography in my books accurate, then insert some made-up places into this framework of realism. But even my fictional Edinburgh locations are inspired by the city's character: its unremarkable eccentricities, its understated strangeness, its hidden nooks and crannies. Maybe there isn't really a little shop in St Stephen Street which appears to sell nothing but shoe polish and has a concealed lift in the basement that'll take you down to a secret intercontinental transport system; but there could be.

Donald Lightwood:

When I lived in the Dean Village I used it as one of the settings for *The Long Revenge*. The story tells of a Highland family evicted from their croft in the 1820s, who make their way to Edinburgh and settle in the village. At that time the Water of Leith was used to power mills and other industries, and so it was easy for the family to find work.

Fortunately for me, King George IV visited Edinburgh in 1822 and Sir Walter Scott arranged sumptuous festivities to celebrate the event. These became part of my story, as did the notorious Burke and Hare, who were living in the Old Town at the time.

Edinburgh is a splendid place for a writer of historical fiction; so much has happened in the city and a great deal of it remains as it was in the past. Simply being there stirs the imagination. Forget the traffic ... and you can picture King George entering St Giles. Stand on the bridge in the Dean Village, and you can hear the water mills churning.

Jonathan Meres:

Writer's Block is a condition that affects all writers at one time or another. Unless they're dead lucky ... or big fibbers! It certainly affects me. I can't think what to write, or which way a story's going to go. Unfortunately, there's no instant remedy. There's no writer's laxative you can take. (If only!)

My own particular way of dealing with it is by going for a run round Arthur's Seat. For me there's no better way of unblocking those creative juices and getting them flowing again. Sometimes I can hardly wait to get home and sit down. In my office I mean.

Stephen Potts:

Edinburgh is a coastal city, but her back is turned to the sea. Her most famous literary son, Robert Louis Stevenson, faced the other way, embracing sea adventures in both his life and his stories. Lesser known, at least in Britain, is John Muir, who grew up in Dunbar, along the North Sea shore, where he spent hours wandering the beaches. After emigrating to the United States he travelled to such places as Yosemite, the Alaskan fjords, and the forests of the Pacific Northwest. He became the foremost naturalist of his day, and wrote extensively about his journeys.

I first learnt of him when hiking through John Muir Woods in California, where mighty redwood trees soar up through the fog, not far from the Pacific breakers and the magnificent Golden Gate Bridge. It was here that my first book, *Hunting Gumnor,* began. I later found another John Muir Wood, much closer to Muir's first home, near Dunbar. Here huge Scots Pines border the sand dunes of a misty North Sea beach, not far from the twin bridges across the Forth. And it was here that *Hunting Gumnor* was finished.

Simon Puttock:

A View with a Room
I chose my first flat in Edinburgh largely because of the view from my sitting room window. It was of the finest drying greens in the city, right at the (not posh) end of Grange Loan, and anyone who disagrees with me had better have something pretty spectacular to back it up with! The green is a vast space, divided into lopsided spaces by stone walls, with flower beds, a couple of old trees and, of course, vast tracts of lawn studded with metal posts (like miniature Victorian lampposts) from which the washing lines are strung ... I need green things to help my stories grow.

Afterword
by Debi Gliori

Debi Gliori, a writer and illustrator, has had a love-hate relationship with the city of Edinburgh, but there is no doubt that it now holds a special place in her heart.

I fled here after my seventeenth birthday to escape from a past that, in my naiveté, I imagined to be tangled beyond repair. Edinburgh, thirty years ago (Am I really that old?) generously offered me a blank page on which I could begin to write myself a whole new history.

Sit down, pet, here's a quill pen and you'll have had your tea?

I defected, then. Went East with my dangerous secrets to seek my fortune, or to allow it to find me. I hated Edinburgh at that time. I was so poor I pressed my face up to lit windows like Hans Christian Andersen's little matchgirl and wished. For what, I cannot remember. Acceptance, I guess. I had a little baby, and smuts from coal fires peppered his pale skin when I walked him in his pram round the streets of the city. I hated it all, then; the cold, the poverty, the grim, grey pursed-mouthness of it, all of the city set in lines of disapproval. But all the while, as I resisted it, Edinburgh was seeping into my heart and my bones; the haar and the wind, the cobbles and fanlights, the hidden wealth and carefully darned tweeds, all of it became part of me. Now, thirty years on, I know that as I fought it, closed my mind to its seductive beauty, shut my eyes against its wide-open skies, Edinburgh had already stolen my heart.

Whichever way I view this city, I'm smitten. From an angel's view; looking down on the city from Turnhouse hilltop in the Pentlands, or a demon's smoky tunnel-vision; looking up at the castle from way down on the train track just before we pull in to Waverley; both are sights to make my spirits soar.

All of what I write and draw has been woven, like a tweed, from the rain and the wind, the grasses and barley fields, the rivers and reeds, the sands and surf and high spaces of this city. Its people have taken me in, trusted me, cherished me and shown me their secret, beating hearts, to which I gladly add my own. I am proud beyond words to belong here and call it home.

Contributors & editors

Gill Arbuthnott was born and brought up in Edinburgh. She left the city briefly during her university years and now teaches biology at Edinburgh Academy. She likes to ground her fantasy in familiar surroundings and so far, all her novels have been set in Scotland. But watch this space ... *The Chaos Clock,* Floris Books; *The Chaos Quest,* Floris Books; *Winterbringers,* Floris Books

Valerie Bierman fell in love with Scottish history — and Edinburgh — when, as a teenager living in Lancashire, she read an extravagantly romantic novel about Mary Queen of Scots. Val founded and ran the Edinburgh Book Festival Children's Fair from 1983 to 1994 and is now a children's book consultant. *Streets Ahead: Tales of City Life* (ed.); *Snake on the Bus and Other Pet Stories* (ed.); *Scary Stories* (ed.)

Sally J. Collins, originally from Wiltshire, has lived and worked as a freelance artist and illustrator in East Lothian since 1988. She has worked closely with a number of Scottish children's writers. *The History of Scotland for Children,* Glowworm Books; Hamish McHaggis series, GW Publishing; *Greyfriars Bobby,* GW Publishing

Robert Dodds (www.robertdodds.com) has worked in England, Mexico and the USA. He set up a degree course in film and television production at Edinburgh College of Art where he still works. *The Midnight Clowns,* Andersen Press; *Nightland,* Andersen Press; *The Secret of Iguando,* Andersen Press

John Fardell was brought up near Bristol and now lives in Edinburgh. He's a freelance cartoonist and illustrator, as well as a writer. His first novel for children, *The Seven Professors of the Far North,* is full of detailed drawings and diagrams. *The Seven Professors of the Far North,* Faber & Faber; *The Flight of the Silver Turtle,* Faber & Faber

Anne Forbes was born in Edinburgh and trained as a teacher. She moved to Kuwait in 1966 and now divides her time between her homes in Scotland and Kuwait. *Dragonfire,* Floris Books; *The Wings of Ruksh,* Floris Books

Lindsey Fraser is a partner in Fraser Ross Associates, a literary agency she co-founded after working for the Scottish Book Trust for many years. Her reviews of children's books appear regularly in the *Sunday Herald.* She was also the manager of Heffers Children's Bookshop in Cambridge.

Vivian French has lived in London, Bristol and now Edinburgh, and she has given talks all over the UK and beyond. She has even led writing workshops in Ibiza and Majorca! She has published around two hundred titles, including poetry, drama and non-fiction, and from picture books to novels for teenagers. *The Daddy Goose Collection,* Chicken House; *The Robe of Skulls,* Walker Books; *Sharp Sheep,* Macmillan

Debi Gliori is the author/illustrator of many picture books for young children. Her series for older readers about the Strega-Borgia family, their outlandish pets and amazing adventures has gained her a worldwide following. Mr Bear series, Orchard; *No Matter What,* Bloomsbury; *Pure Dead ...* series, Corgi

Keith Gray (www.keith-gray.com) was brought up in Grimsby and now lives in Edinburgh. He was anything but a keen reader when he was young, but Robert Westall's book *The Machine Gunners* kick-started his love for stories. *Creepers,* Egmont; *Warehouse,* Red Fox; *The Fearful,* Red Fox

Jan-Andrew Henderson has worked as a fake French waiter, stamp designer, pepper salesman, Easter Bunny and playwright/actor/director at a children's theatre in New York. In 1999 he set up a company running ghost and history tours in Edinburgh. *Secret City,* Oxford University Press; *Hunting Charlie Wilson,* Oxford University Press; *Bunker 10,* Oxford University Press

Diana Hendry writes for all ages, from toddlers to teenagers, as well as for adults. She is also an acclaimed poet. Her novel, *Harvey Angell,* won a Whitbread Award in 1991 and *Harvey Angell Beats Time* won a Scottish Arts Council award. *The Very Noisy Night,* Little Tiger Press; *Harvey Angell,* Red Fox; *You Can't Kiss it Better,* Red Fox

Mollie Hunter is one of Scotland's most popular and influential writers for young people and many of her novels draw on the country's folklore and history. Her books have won numerous awards, including the Carnegie Medal. *The Lothian Run,* Floris Books; *The Thirteenth Member,* Floris Books; *The Spanish Letters,* Floris Books; *A Stranger Came Ashore,* Floris Books

Charlie James graduated from Edinburgh University. She worked as a children's book editor in London and then as a literary agent. She was inspired to write by her children and their friends. *Fish,* Bloomsbury

Jamie Jauncey (www.jauncey.co.uk) has published three novels for young people and has recently written about Robert Louis Stevenson for an adult anthology. Jamie also plays keyboards and sings in a band. *The Albatross Conspiracy,* Scholastic; *The Crystal Keeper,* Scholastic; *The Witness,* Young Picador

Janey Louise Jones (www.princesspoppy. co.uk) first published the Princess Poppy stories herself, writing and illustrating the picture books. The scale of their success led to a major contract with a London publisher. *Princess Poppy: The Birthday,* Picture Corgi; *Princess Poppy: The Wedding,* Picture Corgi; *Princess Poppy: A True Princess,* Young Corgi

Julie Lacome grew up in Fife and has loved drawing, painting and making things for as long as she can remember. She attended Edinburgh College of Art and Central St Martins in London and has always worked as a freelance illustrator — mainly for children's books. *Walking Through the Jungle,* Walker Books; *Ruthie's Big Old Coat,* Walker Books; *Sweetieraptors: A Book o Scots Dinosaurs,* Itchy Coo

Elizabeth Laird (www.elizabethlaird.co.uk) divides her time between Edinburgh and London. She has travelled widely and her experiences and adventures all over the world have informed and inspired her award-winning books. *A Little Piece of Ground,* Macmillan; *Secrets of the Fearless,* Macmillan; *Oranges in No Man's Land,* Macmillan

Donald Lightwood lives in St Andrews and is a former drama adviser in Fife. He dramatized his novel, *The Baillie's Daughter,* and Kathleen

Fidler's *The Desperate Journey* for BBC Scotland Educational Radio. *Don't Forget to Remember,* Scottish Children's Press; *The Long Revenge,* Scottish Children's Press; *The Witches' Mark,* Floris

Joan Lingard is one of our most versatile and best-loved authors. She was born in Edinburgh and lived in Belfast between the ages of two and eighteen. She writes for adults and children of all ages, and is probably best known for the "Kevin and Sadie" quintet set in Northern Ireland. *The Secret of the Black Dagger,* Puffin; *Natasha's Will,* Puffin; *Tilly and the Badgers,* Orchard

Alexander McCall Smith was born in Zimbabwe and was educated there and in Scotland. He is Professor Emeritus of Medical Law at the University of Edinburgh and has written more than sixty books, including the best-selling *The No. 1 Ladies' Detective Agency* and comic adventures for children (www.mccall-smith.com). *Akimbo and the Elephants,* Egmont; *The Five Lost Aunts of Harriet Bean,* Bloomsbury; *The Perfect Hamburger,* Puffin

Jonathan Meres (www.jonathanmeres.co.uk) had a fascinating variety of jobs before finally settling on writing: merchant seaman, ice cream salesman, band member, children's theatre actor and stand-up comedian. *The Big Bad Rumour,* Hutchinson Children's Books, *Yo! Diary!* Piccadilly Press; *Love Dad,* Barrington Stoke

Nicola Morgan was born in a boys' boarding school and taught there by her parents. Her second novel, *Fleshmarket,* won a Scottish Arts Council Award, and *Sleepwalking* was the SAC

Children's Book of the Year 2005. She writes teenage novels, younger children's fiction and non-fiction. *Fleshmarket,* Hodder; *Blame My Brain,* Walker; *The Highwayman's Footsteps,* Walker

Mike Nicholson won the 2005 Kelpies Prize for new Scottish writing with his mystery adventure story, *Catscape* and is currently writing his second novel for children. He loves the idea of mysteries lurking on his doorstep, waiting to be solved. *Catscape,* Floris

Aileen Paterson studied at Edinburgh College of Art and has been a teacher, a studio potter and a craftworker. *Maisie Comes to Morningside* (Three Hills Books) was her first book, and since then the mischievous kitten has starred in more than twenty stories and travelled all over the world. *Maisie's Festival Adventure,* Glowworm Books; *Maisie Bites the Big Apple,* Glowworm Books; *Maisie and the Botanic Garden Mystery,* Royal Botanic Garden Edinburgh

Judy Paterson has lived in Australia and Papua New Guinea. She is now one of Scotland's best-known professional Storytellers, and has travelled the country sharing her stories. *The History of Scotland for Children,* Glowworm Books; *Spook's Guide to Edinburgh* (illustrated by Aileen Paterson), Glowworm Books; *Robert Burns,* Lindsay Publications

Stephen Potts is a consultant psychiatrist at Edinburgh Royal Infirmary. He says that the longer he spends in medicine, the more important his writing becomes. His other great love is the water — most of his adventure stories are set at sea. *Hunting Gumnor,* Egmont; *Compass Murphy,* Egmont; *Abigail's Gift,* Egmont

Simon Puttock was born in New Zealand and grew up in Trinidad, Barbados and England. He has been a DJ and a bookseller and now writes full time. *Horsey,* Egmont; *Little Lost Cowboy,* Oxford University Press; *Don't Count Your Chickens,* Macmillan

Kathryn Ross is a partner in Fraser Ross Associates, a literary agency she co-founded with Lindsey Fraser after working for the Scottish Book Trust for many years. They consult on many literary projects, including the Pushkin Prizes in Scotland and the Blue Peter Book Awards. Her reviews of children's books appear regularly in the *Scotsman,* and she used to teach English in schools in the UK and Germany.

J.K. Rowling (www.jkrowling.com) grew up in Chepstow and studied French and Classics at Exeter University. She started writing the Harry Potter series during a train journey from Manchester to London, and completed the first book when she came to live in Edinburgh. *Harry Potter and the Philosopher's Stone,* Bloomsbury; *Harry Potter and the Prisoner of Azkaban,* Bloomsbury; *Harry Potter and the Half-Blood Prince,* Bloomsbury

Linda Strachan (www.lindastrachan.com) was born in Edinburgh to Scottish/Italian parents. She had various jobs after leaving school, including being a bacteriology laboratory technician and a model. She has written around fifty children's books. *What Colour is Love?* Bloomsbury; the Hamish McHaggis series, GW Publishing; *Greyfriars Bobby,* GW Publishing

Books mentioned in the text

NB: OP means the book is currently out of print, but is available through libraries

Catscape (Floris Books, 2005), Mike Nicholson: Fergus and Murdo become embroiled in a mystery in which cats are disappearing from the streets of Stockbridge — and that is by no means the only strange thing going on in the area.

The Chaos Clock (Floris Books, 2003), Gill Arbuthnott: Kate and David live quite ordinary lives until they are drawn into a terrifying struggle between the Lords of Chaos and the Guardians of Time.

A Child's Garden of Verses (various editions, 1895), Robert Louis Stevenson: A classic poetry collection.

The Dark Shadow (Floris Books, first published 1989), Mary Rhind: Lizzie is hopeful that a visit to St Triduana's Well in Restalrig might cure her blindness. Instead, she and her brother find themselves caught up in the troubles surrounding the Reformation.

Dragonfire (Floris Books, 2006), Anne Forbes: Arthur's Seat may seem like an ordinary Edinburgh hill, but in this entertaining fantasy it is alive with activity and a cast of extraordinary characters — including a dragon.

An Edinburgh Reel (OP, 1975), Iona McGregor: John Murray returns to Edinburgh, determined to rebuild his life with his daughter, Marion, following the failure of the '45 Jacobite rebellion.

Fish (Bloomsbury, 2006), Charlie James: A comic adventure about a boy who turns into a cod with remarkable ease — which is fine until he comes into close contact with a killer whale ...

Fleshmarket (Hodder Children's Books, 2003), Nicola Morgan: Robbie is haunted by his mother's horrific death, and determined to wreak revenge on Knox, the nineteenth-century Edinburgh surgeon he holds responsible.

The Flight of the Silver Turtle (Faber, 2006), John Fardell: Ben, Zara, Sam and Marcia help the eccentric Amy McAirdrie build her homemade plane, little knowing that a suspect organization — Noctarma — has other plans for the them.

A Flute in Mayferry Street (Floris Books, first published 1976), Eileen Dunlop: An intriguing mystery set in a New Town House, in which the tragedies of the past are revealed and finally resolved.

Greyfriars Bobby (GW Publishing, 2006), Linda Strachan and Sally J. Collins: An illustrated retelling of the story of the plucky little dog who never forgot his master.

Hamish McHaggis series (GW Publishing, 2005), Linda Strachan and Sally J. Collins: Take a tour of Scotland in a series of adventures featuring Hamish and his wildlife friends.

High House (OP, 1972), Honor Arundel: Emma adapts to a new life with her eccentric Aunt Patsy in a top flat in Edinburgh's Old Town, following the death of her parents.

Hunting Gumnor (Egmont Books, 1999), Stephen Potts: Gumnor, the last of a whale-type species, has acted as a foghorn from the harbour for as long as Rarty can remember. But then Gumnor disappears ...

The Long Revenge (Scottish Children's Press, 2002), Donald Lightwood: Two brothers are forced into a lawless life in Edinburgh following the horrors of eviction from their Highland home during the Clearances.

The Lothian Run (Floris Books, first published 1970), Mollie Hunter: Eighteenth-century Scotland is awash with intrigue and danger. This thriller combines a story of audacious smuggling with an attempt to relaunch the Jacobite campaign.

The Maisie Books (Three Hills Books, Glowworm Books, 1984 onwards), Aileen Paterson: Maisie the kilted kitten takes centre stage in a series of books, one of the most recent of which is set in Edinburgh's Royal Botanic Gardens.

The Midnight Clowns (Andersen Press, 2000), Robert Dodds: Ben and Claire become the target of a troupe of supernatural clowns in this mystery.

Peter Pan (first published as *Peter and Wendy)* (various editions, 1911), J.M. Barrie: The classic story of the boy who refused to grow up.

The Prime of Miss Jean Brodie (Penguin, 1969), Muriel Spark: The modern classic about a charismatic teacher in a girls' school in 1930s Edinburgh.

Rags and Riches (OP, 1988), Joan Lingard: Seb and Sam find a coat with a silver lining in their mother's second-hand clothes shop. Could their luck be about to change?

Remembrance (Random House Children's Books, 2002), Theresa Breslin: The story of a small Borders community where a way of life is changed forever by World War I.

Secret City (Oxford University Press, 2004), Jan-Andrew Henderson: Charlie comes to Edinburgh with his parents who are taking part in the Festival, leaving him with time to explore ...

Secrets of the Fearless (Macmillan Children's Books, 2005), Elizabeth Laird: A breathtaking thriller set in the nineteenth century, which begins in Leith with twelve-year-old John Barr press-ganged to join the navy.

The Sign of the Black Dagger (Puffin Books, 2005), Joan Lingard: Set in the present day and eighteenth-century Edinburgh, two sets of children — past and present — must solve the mystery of their respective fathers' disappearance.

A Sound of Chariots (OP, 1972), Mollie Hunter: An autobiographical novel about a girl growing up in East Lothian.

The Spanish Letters (Floris Books, first published 1964), Mollie Hunter: It's 1589, and the Spanish king, with some Scottish earls, plots to capture James IV and invade England.

The Strange Case of Dr Jekyll and Mr Hyde (various editions, 1886), Robert Louis Stevenson: The classic split-personality horror story.

The Thing That Mattered Most (Scottish Poetry Library/B&W, 2006), edited by Julie Johnstone: A beautifully-illustrated collection of poems for young people by Scottish poets.

The Thirteenth Member (Floris Books, first published 1974), Mollie Hunter: A stirring story of witchcraft and treason set in Edinburgh and East Lothian in the sixteenth century.

Treasure Island (various editions, 1883), Robert Louis Stevenson: The classic adventure tale of buccaneers and buried gold.

The Wind in the Willows (various editions, 1908), Kenneth Grahame: The classic story of life on the riverbank.

You Can't Kiss it Better (Red Fox, 2003), Diana Hendry: A group of youngsters deals with being in a foster family in Edinburgh.

Organizations and visitor attractions

BRAW and Scottish Book Trust; For information about writers, illustrators, reading and books; www.braw.org.uk; www.scottishbooktrust.com

City of Edinburgh Libraries; You'll find all the books mentioned here through your local library; www.edinburgh.gov.uk/libraries

The Edinburgh International Book Festival; Seventeen days of author events every August; www.edbookfest.co.uk

Edinburgh UNESCO City of Literature; The organisation at the centre of Edinburgh's literary activities; www.cityofliterature.com

The Scottish Poetry Library, tel. 0131 557 2876, www.spl.org.uk

The Scottish Storytelling Centre, tel. 0131 556 9579, www.scottishstorytellingcentre.co.uk

The Writers' Museum, tel. 0131 529 4901, www.cac.org.uk

Mary King's Close, tel. 08702 430160, www.realmarykingsclose.com

The Museum of Childhood, tel. 0131 529 4142, www.cac.org.uk

The Museum of Edinburgh, tel. 0131 529 4143, www.cac.org.uk

The National Gallery of Scotland, tel. 0131 624 6200, www.natgalscot.ac.uk

The National Library of Scotland, tel. 0131 623 3700, www.nls.uk

The National Museums of Scotland, tel. 0131 247 4422, www.nms.ac.uk

The National Portrait Gallery, tel. 0131 624 6200, www.natgalscot.ac.uk

Our Dynamic Earth, tel. 0131 550 7800, www.dynamicearth.co.uk

The Palace of Holyrood House, tel. 0131 556 5100, www.royal.gov.uk

The People's Story, tel. 0131 529 4057, www.cac.org.uk

The Royal Botanic Gardens, tel. 0131 552 7171, www.rbge.org.uk

The Royal College of Surgeons, tel. 0131 527 1649

St Giles Cathedral, www.stgilescathedral.org.uk

The Scott Monument, tel. 0131 529 4068, www.cac.org.uk

The Scottish Parliament, Visitor Services, tel. 0131 348 5200

Acknowledgments

The publishers wish to thank the following for permission to reproduce copyright material:

Gill Arbuthnott for the extracts from *The Chaos Clock* © Gill Arbuthnott, 2003.

Theresa Breslin for the extract from *Remembrance* © Theresa Breslin, 2002, by permission of Random House Children's Books, and Laura Cecil Literary Agency.

Eileen Dunlop for the extract from *A Flute in Mayferry Street* © Eileen Dunlop, 1976.

John Fardell for the extract from *The Flight of the Silver Turtle* © John Fardell, 2006, by permission of Faber and Faber.

Anne Forbes for extracts from *Dragonfire* © Anne Forbes, 2006.

Stephanie Green for the extract from 'Embra Buses' from *The Thing That Mattered Most* © Stephanie Green, 2006.

Jan-Andrew Henderson for extracts from *Secret City* © Jan-Andrew Henderson, 2004, by permission of Oxford University Press.

Diana Hendry for extracts from *You Can't Kiss It Better.* © Diana Hendry, 2003 by permission of Random House Children's Books.

Mollie Hunter for extracts from *The Spanish Letters, The Lothian Run, The Thirteenth Member* and *A Sound of Chariots.* © Mollie Hunter, 1964, 1970, 1972, 1974.

Elizabeth Laird for extracts from *Secrets of the Fearless* © Elizabeth Laird, 2005, by permission of Macmillan Children's Books.

Joan Lingard for extracts from *Rags and Riches* and *The Sign of the Black Dagger* © Joan Lingard, 1988, 2005 by permission of the author.

Nicola Morgan for the extracts from *Fleshmarket.* © Nicola Morgan, 2003, by permission of Hodder and Stoughton Ltd.

Mike Nicholson for the extracts from *Catscape.* © Mike Nicholson, 2005.

Aileen Paterson for the extracts from *Maisie Comes to Morningside* © Aileen Paterson, 1984, by permission of Three Hills Books.

Mary Rhind for the extract from *The Dark Shadow* © Mary Rhind, 1988.

Linda Strachan for the extracts from *Greyfriars Bobby* © Linda Strachan, 2006, by permission of GW Publishing.

Photography credits

p.6: Ove Tøpfer; pp.20/21: Abdul Nusrat; p.23: Erin Calaway-Mackay; p.27: andyconniecox; p.32: Martin Burns; p.33: Dave Challis; p.36: Mel Cameron-Radford; p.37: John McDermott; p.40: Ross D. Wood; p.48: Colin Angus Mackay; p.51: Billy Rosendale; p.77: Marco Varisco

Illustration credits

p.30: Julie Lacome; p.35: Sally J. Collins from *Greyfriars Bobby;* p.55: Harriet Buckley; p.64: Aileen Paterson; all other illustrations by Adrian B. McMurchie

Index